BRITISH RAIL THE FIRST 25 YEARS

BRITISH RAIL
The First 25 Years

MICHAEL R. BONAVIA
MA PhD FCIT

DAVID & CHARLES

Newton Abbot   London   North Pomfret (Vt)

British Library Cataloguing in Publication Data
Bonavia, Michael Robert
  British Rail.
  1. British Railways — History
  I. Title
  385'.0941   HE3020.B/   80-41448
  ISBN 0-7153-8002-8

Typeset by TJB Photosetting, Grantham, Lincs and
Printed in Great Britain
by A. Wheaton & Co Ltd, Hennock Road, Exeter
for David & Charles (Publishers) Limited
Brunel House   Newton Abbot   Devon

Published in the United States of America
by David & Charles Inc
North Pomfret   Vermont 05053   USA

Contents

Preface and Acknowledgements

This book is in no sense an official history. I have not asked for or been given any sponsorship or facilities from the British Railways Board, and what follows is essentially a subjective view of a quarter-century of railway progress, coloured in places by personal impressions of individuals as well as of policies.

My qualifications for attempting the rather daunting task of covering such a vast subject in a single book of modest length must rely mainly upon a varied experience. I was among the first handful of railway company officers recruited, shortly before nationalisation, to the embryo British Transport Commission; subsequently I also served the Railway Executive, the Eastern Region and the British Railways Board. I have thus had opportunities to see some of the more controversial railway policies from more than one viewpoint.

To compare the quarter-century following nationalisation (1948-72) with the equal life-span of the pre-nationalisation companies (1923-1948) is not easy, because the world outside the railways has been changing so quickly. The companies certainly enjoyed a prestige, an influence in the worlds of business and politics, that is denied to British Rail. I have tried elsewhere (*) to suggest the characteristics of the LMS, LNER, GWR and SR. The companies were sometimes perhaps over-conservative and slow to react to changing forces in the outside world. On the other hand, they were usually consistent and effective in the execution of policies, once these had been determined, and they enjoyed the great advantages of continuity in their top management. Sir James Milne was General Manager of the Great Western Railway for 22 years; Sir Herbert Walker of the Southern, Sir Ralph Wedgwood of the LNER and Lord Stamp of the LMS were each chief executives of their railways for over 16 years. But after nationalisation the chairmen of British Rail numbered seven in 25 years — an average tenure of less than four years.

And there have been four major Acts of Parliament, each drastically changing the organisation, powers and duties of British Railways, as well as several minor Acts, in these 25 years. A symptom of this is that

* In *The Four Great Railways* (David & Charles, 1980)

7

my local station, which from 1923 to 1948 exhibited notices under the single heading of 'Southern Railway', between 1948 and 1972 at times showed such information under the headings of: The Railway Executive; British Transport Commission; British Railways; Southern Region; or British Railways Board.

So there has been chopping and changing on a scale unknown before. Some may argue that this is a healthy sign, warding off any tendency to lethargy or complacency. Certainly at the top level there has been a constant ferment of ideas, many good and some less good, throughout the period. On the debit side is the undoubted fact that change and uncertainty have prevented the expected benefits from many policies being realised, simply because a new policy has been adopted before there has been time for the old policy to be fully implemented. The critics of the railways seldom understand the frustrations and handicaps — investment cut-backs, rising costs, labour disputes, political intervention — under which BR managements have laboured since 1948, far greater than anything experienced in company days. But the quality of management has not declined; on the contrary, those who were recruited from outside in the 1950s and 1960s were surprised to discover that BR's problems were far more intricate, and the quality of management was far better than they had been led to expect.

The story ends on a more hopeful note. The first few years after 1948 were certainly rather backward-looking; the management was trying to restore the pre-war state of the railways within the framework of nationalised transport. Then came several years of uncertainty, with a painful readjustment to the post-war situation, embracing the Modernisation Plan and the Beeching Re-shaping. Finally there emerged the slimmed-down, much-changed BR of the 1970s, harnessing advanced technology to the performance of redefined tasks. This is not to imply that everything done in the early years was misconceived, or that every decision in recent times has been 100 per cent correct; progress, nevertheless, sometimes hesitant and sometimes rapid, towards a realistic concept of the railway's role in the economy, has been continuous.

I am greatly in the debt of friends and former colleagues (and chiefs also) who have read portions of my text in draft and commented helpfully upon them; in particular (in alphabetical order) Sir John Elliot, Derek Fowler, Frank Harding, Leslie Harrington, Edgar Larkin, Robert Long, Charles McLeod, Philip Satchwell and David Williams. But the responsibility for any remaining errors or omissions, and for all expressions of opinion, is mine alone.

M.R. Bonavia

Chapter 1
Four into One Must Go

New Year's Day had not yet in 1948 been declared a public holiday in England and Wales. So on Thursday 1 January the morning trains carried their usual complement of commuters to work, apart from those who were suffering from too severe a hangover from the previous night's celebrations. Some revellers may have heard at midnight, among the other noises announcing the New Year, the whistles sounded by engine drivers which were not merely saluting 1948 but also the nationalisation of the railways.

In some railway compartments the conversation must have turned on the changeover and a few jocular or perhaps over-optimistic travellers were reported to have argued with ticket collectors that as the new shareholders they ought not to have to pay to travel on their own railways.

Of outward differences little was to be seen. One or two sombre posters had appeared headed 'British Transport Commission' or 'Transport Act 1947'; but it was to be some weeks before the first locomotive was observed bearing the legend 'British Railways' on its tender or tank sides.

If passengers saw little immediate change, so did the staff. The same stationmasters, inspectors, gangers and foremen were in charge. Even higher up, in the District offices, the formal responsibilities were usually the same. It was only at chief departmental officer level that the impact was immediate; it took time for the effects of change to filter down, and for the consequences of the disappearance of the companies to be grasped.

That chilly January morning also saw a press photographer taking a picture of Sir Cyril Hurcomb walking across St James's Park to the offices of the British Transport Commission in the London Transport headquarters building, known as 55 Broadway, above St James's Park Underground station. Almost at the same time, Sir Eustace Missenden was arriving by car at the former Great Central Hotel building, now known as 222 Marylebone Road, the offices of the Railway Executive. Two chairmen were settling into their new posts and, so far as the public was concerned, it was a mystery as to which of them was really in command of the railways. All that was clear was that the Great Western, the London Midland & Scottish, the London & North Eastern and the Southern Railway companies had been replaced by a Commission, an Executive, and a number of Regions.

Organisational changes and administrative procedures are very important to those personally affected by them, but often very boring to everyone else. But, to understand just how British Railways was created, some of the formal steps need to be recalled.

The Transport Bill, 1946, became the Transport Act, 1947 on receiving the royal assent on 6 August 1947. It swept up the main line railways and some 50 smaller companies — many controlling joint lines or stations — simply by 'vesting' them in the British Transport Commission as from 1 January 1948, and providing that compensation should be paid to the shareholders on scales laid down by the Act for exchange into British Transport stock, a Government-guaranteed security. The Act also provided that all privately-owned railway wagons, of which there were some half a million, should be compulsorily acquired. Here the compensation was set out in a lengthy table, the amounts varying between £16.10s (£16.50) for an 8-ton wagon built in 1902 or earlier and £414 for a 21-ton all-steel wagon built in 1946.

But several small standard gauge railways were not absorbed under the vesting process — the Easingwold, Liverpool Overhead, North Sunderland, Swansea & Mumbles, Corringham Light, and Derwent Valley Light, as well as some narrow-gauge lines such as the Romney, Hythe & Dymchurch. As regards the way in which the nationalised railways were to be managed, the Act merely said that the Commission had a general duty 'to provide .... an efficient, adequate, economical and properly integrated system of public inland transport and port facilities within Great Britain'; that there should be 'public authorities known as Executives to assist the Commission in the discharge of their functions' and that there should be a Railway Executive which should, like the other Executives, 'exercise such functions of the Commission as are delegated to them' under a scheme approved by the Minister.

To get things moving, the Commission made a Scheme of Delegation empowering the Executive to act as though it had all the powers of the former railway companies *except* as provided in BTC Directions limiting these powers. These Directions, when issued, related mainly to capital expenditure on new works or renewal programmes, appointment of senior railway officers, and national agreements with the unions on wages, salaries and conditions.

But — and this is the oddity — although the Executive was rather like a subsidiary company and the Commission like the holding company in a big financial group, the Act said that 'all the business carried on by the Commission .... shall form one undertaking and the Commission shall so conduct that undertaking and .... levy such fares rates and other charges as to secure that the revenue of the Commission is not less than sufficient .... for the meeting of charges properly chargeable to revenue, taking one year with another'. All this meant was, that although the railways had their own management, they were under the financial control of the Commission and in particular were not able to fix their own charges, which had to be related to the Commission's duty to break even.

With the forthcoming disappearance of the private companies, decisions had to be reached on what was to replace them. It was quickly decided that below the Executive there must be managements known as Regions, but the nature and the number of these were not immediately agreed. As late as October 1947 discussions were taking place as to whether eventually there might be eight regions, namely:-

Southern
Western
Welsh
Scottish
ex-LMS (part, centred on Manchester)
ex-LMS (southern part)
ex-LNER (part, centred on York)
ex-LNER (southern part)

Thereafter for a time it was thought that five Regions would be appropriate — one each replacing respectively the Southern Railway, the Great Western Railway, the London Midland & Scottish Railway in England and Wales, and the London & North Eastern Railway south of the Border, and lastly — partly no doubt on political grounds — a single Region embracing the Scottish portions of the LMS and the LNER. But the decision was taken that the decentralised character of the LNER organisation made it appropriate to set up two separate Regions replacing the Southern Area and the North Eastern Area of the LNER.

By the beginning of November therefore six Regions had been decided upon, apart from a question which the Executive agreed to examine, namely whether there should be separate Regions for Wales and for North-West England. (It can be mentioned here that by the middle of 1948 both of these possibilities were ruled out for the time being by agreement between the Commission and the Executive.)

The fact that many minor 'railway undertakings' were being taken over involved their allocation to one or more of the new Regions. Thus the London Midland Region included the Mersey Railway and the Cheshire Lines Committee. The Eastern Region included the Midland & Great Northern Joint Railway; the Southern Region included the Somerset & Dorset Joint Railway. The Scottish Region presented some special difficulties because of the need to amalgamate the ex-LMS and ex-LNER systems North of the Border.

The Regions varied considerably in size. At the vesting date, their route mileages were:-

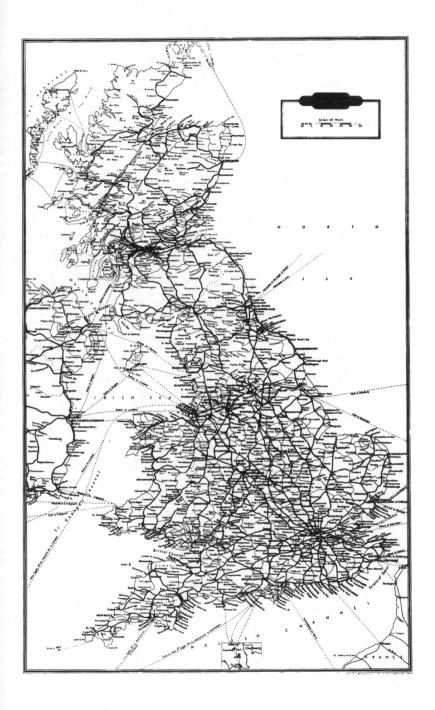

London Midland	4,993 route miles
Western	3,782 " "
Scottish	3,730 " "
Eastern	2,836 " "
Southern	2,250 " "
North Eastern	1,823 " "

From the outset the name 'British Railways' was applied to the whole system, though it had no legal status, not being mentioned in the Transport Act. The name 'Region' also was not a legal title. Some people felt (and some still do) that it is not very appropriate for a railway system or network. Why not six 'railways', under the central Executive? In fact representations were made in 1947 to Hurcomb through the Minister that 'Region' was an official term used in other contexts — the most important being the sub-division of the country for emergency civil government purposes — and should not be applied in a nationalised industry. Hurcomb brushed this objection aside, saying that the use of 'Region' had already started, and it was too late to change.

Thus, towards the end of 1947 the future organisation had taken shape as follows:

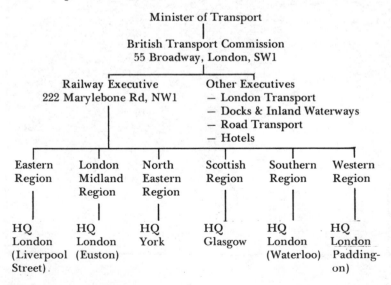

Some sections of former main line railways were to be transferred to London Transport in a preliminary tidying up operation. The Eastern Region handed over the ex-GER lines operated by London Transport's Central Line, and the Western Region the Ealing & Shepherd's Bush and North Acton to Greenford sections, also operated by Central Line trains.

Between the passing of the Act in August and the end of the year there was pretty feverish activity. Members were designated to take up office in both the Commission and the Executive on 1 January 1948; the chief personalities involved will be described in the next chapter. An immediate problem was where the two bodies concerned with the nationalised railways should have their headquarters. The Commission was intended to be a small, policy-making organisation. Its Chairman, Sir Cyril Hurcomb, had been a life-long civil servant and felt more at home in the neighbourhood of Whitehall than in, for example, any railway office. Lord Ashfield, who was retiring from the Chairmanship of London Transport to join the Commission, was equally disinclined to leave his sumptuous panelled office in the London Transport headquarters building over St James's Park station. He offered Hurcomb the use of two floors in 55 Broadway — as the LT building was officially known — and this was readily accepted by the BTC's future chairman who wrote complacently in the Commission's first annual report that its office was 'in sight of the centre of government'.

This accommodation consisted of two upper floors, the eight and ninth, divided up by metal and glass partitions, not at all to the liking of the former railway officers who had been drafted into the Commission and who felt that a prestige office would have been more appropriate for the headquarters of an undertaking of such vast size and importance. An unsuspecting clerk allocating rooms in these rather spartan surroundings innocently designated one for Lord Ashfield's use, which the great man contemptuously rejected, retaining his own prestige suite on the seventh floor — rather to the discomfiture of his successor as Chairman of London Transport, Lord Latham, who had to use makeshift accommodation until Lord Ashfield's death in November 1948.

Hurcomb's satisfaction with this accommodation reflected his own austere taste. But the Commission's stark and unimpressive office undoubtedly played some part, even if a minor one, in the general feeling of contempt for the nominally senior body that was common among the staff of the Railway Executive. At 55 Broadway even the railway tradition of a mess for senior staff did not hold good, though eventually London Transport provided luncheon facilities (on a cash basis!) which was regarded more as a canteen than a proper 'mess', and was not an acceptable means of offering hospitality after business meetings in the accepted railway manner. So the Commission's officers felt rather like poor relations of the more suitably housed Executive staff.

The Executive, being organised on functional lines, with members exercising direct control over most departmental activities in the whole railway system, was clearly going to need much more accommodation than the Commission, and it was determined to make itself reasonably comfortable. The obvious choice would seem to be one of the railway headquarters buildings in London. But on examination none seemed really suitable or easily available. Starting with the LMS, Euston's shabby, dusty corridors certainly led to some rooms of dignity; there was a touch of faded grandeur about the double staircase curving out of the Great Hall and leading to the two sets of offices known respectively as 'The Chairman's side' and 'The President's side'. But these in total were inadequate, and the alternative building, Euston House, although a modern, 1930s-style office block housing the traffic departments, was — owing to the centralisation of the LMS — still essential to the running of the railway.

Paddington had had its General Offices almost cut in two by wartime bombs, and its long corridors and old-fashioned layout made it quite impracticable for transformation into a modern office. In any case, it was the focus of opposition to nationalisation! Its main attraction lay in the splendid collection of historic pictures and models along the corridors, which a later General Manager of the Western Region, declaring 'I don't want to work in a museum', unceremoniously chucked out — something for which many find it hard to forgive him.

The Southern also, despite its seven London termini, had little to offer. Waterloo's General Offices had had its General Manager's suite bombed; after the war the GM had to take over the former Traffic Manager's accommodation. London Bridge, still housing some departments, had been very severely damaged indeed.

The LNER had scattered its departments among its three termini. Since 1945 it had in addition a small Chief General Manager's office in two adapted houses in Dorset Square, adjacent to Marylebone station. But King's Cross, the pre-war seat of the Chief General Manager, had suffered severe bomb damage; the Marylebone offices, apart from those of the Chairman and Secretary, were cramped, and reflected the poverty of the Great Central, which had run out of money after the London Extension had reached Marylebone.

Liverpool Street, the home of the Divisional General Manager, Southern Area, would have to become the Eastern Region headquarters. A solution however was found by the LNER, not perhaps unconnected with the fact that that railway's Assistant General Manager (Works and General) had been designated as the future Chief Officer (New Works) of the Railway Executive.

The Hotel Great Central, opposite Marylebone Station, was only in very partial use as a trainmen's hostel at the time. Its history had been curious. Built by a syndicate headed by Sir Blundell Maple after the Great Central Railway had completed its London Extension, it had never really been numbered among the leading railway hotels such as the Charing Cross or the Great Western Royal. But it was comfortable and relatively inexpensive; it had been advertising in 1903 inclusive terms (ie full pension) from 15s (75p) per day! It boasted an Oak Room with fake Old Master oil paintings on the panelled walls, as well as (of course) a Winter Garden where a string orchestra played in the afternoons to the rattle of teacups.

During the second world war it was requisitioned for use as a transit centre for troops, particularly Canadians, passing through London. Its dilapidated state at the end of the war did not however discourage the LNER from buying it for £500,000 (a lot more than the Great Central would have had to pay) with the intention of using it to rehouse clerical staff, particularly in the Chief Accountant's office, returning from their evacuation accommodation. But the Government of the day was determined to restrict office use of buildings and the LNER was obliged to utilise the hotel as a trainmen's hostel for the time being.

The size of the building made it attractive to the future Executive and, with nationalisation imminent, the Government was easily persuaded to issue the permit for office use by a state corporation which had just been refused to a private company.

Not all the building was brought into use, but the members of the Executive were allotted spacious first-floor rooms far superior to anything occupied by the Commission; a certain amount of necessary cleaning and redecoration was carried out and, again a contrast to the BTC, messes for senior and junior officers were available from the start. Accordingly, if morale depends on a feeling that the chiefs have some regard to the comfort of their subordinates, the Executive scored handsomely in this respect over the Commission.

There was not much difficulty in deciding upon the headquarters of each new Region. Euston station (with some departments housed in nearby Euston House) was obviously right for the London Midland, as was Paddington for the Western, and Waterloo for the Southern. On the Eastern, Liverpool Street saw a simple transition from being the office of the Divisional General Manager to the headquarters of the Eastern Region. There were some complications for the two

18

Regions being carved out of the LNER in England, because that company had some 'all-line' departments; for the time being these continued to be joint between the Eastern and North Eastern Regions. They included the Solicitor, the Accountant, the Chief Mechanical Engineer, the Electrical Engineer and the Stores Superintendent. The Chief General Manager's small office in Dorset Square disappeared completely in the new organisation.

At York, the North Eastern Region painlessly took over the splendid office building originally built by Horace Field in the 'free Georgian style' for the North Eastern Railway, and which later became the LNER North Eastern Area Headquarters. In Scotland, however, the LNER Divisional General Manager's office in the old North British Railway Edinburgh headquarters was abandoned in favour of premises in Buchanan Street, Glasgow near the ex-Caledonian station.

The actual 'vesting' was accomplished with a minimum of ostentation on the management side — a contrast to the National Coal Board's 1946 hoisting of flags marked 'NCB' at every coal mine on vesting day! The shadow Railway Executive issued documents headed 'RE Instruction No 1 to Officers in the Regions', for all former company officers who needed to know what their new responsibilities were and to whom they should report. For the most part, the responsibilities were those of their former company posts, except that, as already mentioned, various joint lines and minor 'railway undertakings' now came within one of the new Regions.

So the changeover took place comparatively smoothly, at least on the surface. Below the surface there were many tensions. Some of those who joined the Executive headquarters organisation had been pressed to do so by chiefs who were themselves moving 'upstairs' as members or chief officers; others volunteered, hoping for more authority and more scope for initiative at the higher level.

Among those who remained in the regional offices the mood was partly apprehensive, partly hostile to those who had left. The word 'traitor' was occasionally applied to a departed colleague. As for the handful who had joined the Commission, they were regarded as having left the railway service and become some sort of civil servant.

So far as the rank and file were concerned, while there seemed to be no immediate change in their work, those who were keen union members were pleased that nationalisation marked the conclusion of a campaign waged for many years by the railway trade unions. On the Sunday following the changeover, the National Union of Railwaymen held mass meetings in many large railway centres. More than 2,000 railwaymen attended the London meeting in a West End theatre, addressed by the Union's President. A circular to District Councils and Branch Secretaries dated 8 December 1947 reported that the Executive Committee would arrange for a speaker — a member of the EC, a union official, or an NUR-sponsored Member of Parliament — to be present at any celebration meeting that might be arranged locally. The management had agreed that meetings might be held on railway premises where suitable, provided there was no dislocation of work.

Meetings were of different types. Apart from the large meeting in the London Coliseum, at the Belle Vue circus in Manchester the New Year was celebrated by the arrival in the ring of the Railway Queen, drawn by a miniature railway locomotive. A 'Grand Gala Dance' was arranged by Paddington No 3 Branch: Peterborough and Darlington held 'socials and dances', Stourbridge No 1 Branch a smoking concert. Other celebrations took place at Hull, Stratford, Pontypridd, Newport (Mon), Birmingham, Newcastle, Swansea and Cardiff. The latter was marked by a speech from Mr. L.J. Callaghan, then Parliamentary Secretary to the Ministry of Transport, in which he argued that 'we ought to have an annual Railway Day' to celebrate nationalisation.

The NUR's journal, the *Railway Review*, recalled in a leader on 2 January 1948 that the campaign for nationalisation of the railways had really been started by the former Amalgamated Society of Railway Servants in 1911, even though 16 years earlier the Trades Union Congress had passed a resolution advocating the same object. It insisted that the railway workers now expected to participate in the management and control of the nationalised service.

A month earlier, however, a sour note had been struck in an article by F.V. Pickstock entitled 'Government by "Experts" — End of Any Ideas of Workers' Control'. It severely criticised appointments that had already been announced of the future heads of British Railways, arguing that 'the workers have exchanged capitalists for "experts" ', and that the appointments should not have been made 'with an eye to technical knowledge of railway work' but 'because of their capacity for tackling the enormous human, social and semi-political problems of organising an industry of over 600,000 workers'.

But the official line was quite hopeful; the NUR President's New Year message expressed the belief 'that the policy being pursued by the Government will be successful, providing we all pull together — and in this direction our Movement can and will, I hope, be a tower of strength'.

A more sober view was taken by the Railway Clerks' Association, which published in its *Railway Service Journal* a leading article by the General Secretary headed 'We Start Afresh', welcoming the new organisation but warning that 'it would be foolish to entertain the idea that as from the vesting date all will be well'. The General Secretary appealed for more consultation between management and staff, arguing that 'in the past any sense of community of interest between the two sides of the industry was destroyed by the feeling that the staff were paid to do as they were told and were not expected to think. These days have passed, but joint consultation is even now not a reality. It is often conceded in principle but withheld in spirit'.

By the middle of 1948 the first visible signs could be noticed by rail users that unification of the system was a reality, with the use of the title 'British Railways' on locomotives, on station notices and in press advertisements. The Regional organisation was given public emphasis by adoption of a totem derived remotely from the London Transport bulls-eye but more rudely described as a pair of inter-twined sausages, in new Regional colours:

London Midland:	red (alas, a muddy maroon, not Midland red)
Eastern:	dark blue (vaguely GER)
North Eastern:	tangerine (a puzzle to everyone)
Western:	brown (more or less GWR chocolate)
Southern:	green (not the SR Malachite)
Scottish:	light blue (from the St Andrew's cross, or vaguely Caledonian Railway)

These outward signs had very little to do with the major problems faced by the new Executive. First came the difficulties of coping with heavy traffics, despite run-down equipment still suffering from wartime over-use and under-maintenance. Next came the need to use the resources of the new system as a whole, to rationalise and standardise for the sake of economy. Last, the Commission was charged with 'integrating' the public transport system, and just what the Railway Executive's part was in this was quite uncertain.

But before describing how these tasks were tackled it is appropriate to mention the personalities who were now in charge, replacing the Chairmen, Directors and General Managers who had controlled railway development and railway policy for so many years.

Chapter 2
Men on the Job

No one, before Sir Eustace Missenden, could have claimed to be the head of all the main line railways of Great Britain. However, even when he assumed the Chairmanship of the Railway Executive, he did not become an autocrat like Sir Edward Watkin, nor even a super-General Manager like Lord Stamp, the former President of the LMS. The civil servants and politicians who designed the new organisation had intended top policy to be settled by the British Transport Commission, leaving technical questions and detailed management to the Executive. And they did not want the head of the Executive to be a powerful force, but merely a co-ordinator and spokesman for the experts who were to run each department for the railways as a whole.

All this might sound logical on paper; it did not work out very well in practice. Personality clashes inevitably arose and played a significant part; and the personality of Missenden was certainly an important element.

When the appointment of a Chairman was being considered, one of the General Managers from a former company seemed the obvious choice. Sir James Milne of the GWR, of which he had been GM since 1929, was both liked and respected. Of the others, Sir William Wood, President of the Executive of the LMS since 1941, was earmarked for membership of the BTC; while the LNER's acting Chief General Manager, Miles Beevor, was designated as the future Chief Secretary and Legal Adviser of the Commission. Missenden had been the forceful and often ruthless Southern Railway GM since 1941, but he was not really a man of the world, or known in political circles, in the same way as Milne.

Milne was 65 years old, and he was far from enthusiastic

about nationalisation, to say the least, but he might have taken the Chairmanship if he had been allowed to retain some outside directorships. The Directors of the GWR, incidentally, had elected him to a seat on the Board which he had not been able to take up because the Minister of War Transport had ruled that this would be incompatible with his membership of the Railway Executive Committee; one could not serve both God (the Minister) and Mammon (the shareholders)! This principle was extended to the Chairmanship of the RE, so that Milne stepped aside and Missenden was offered the Chairmanship. He accepted it, though with the private intention of retiring before too long. Son of a South Eastern & Chatham Railway stationmaster, he was a very competent railwayman, experienced more on the operating than the commercial side, and very loyal to the practices of the Southern Railway. He was a good organiser and knew how to delegate; he looked after the interests of those subordinates who had served him well. He firmly declined to work over-long hours and was careful, perhaps even fussy, over his health. He lacked both the warm, extrovert personality of his precedessor at Waterloo, Gilbert Szlumper, and the intellectual and managerial distinction of Sir Herbert Walker (to whom he had given great admiration); he did not move easily in Government circles, being suspicious of both politicians and civil servants.

He found himself out of his element in trying to co-ordinate a team of Executive Members who were in no way responsible to him in the way that railway departmental officers had been responsible to a General Manager. The method by which the team had been chosen had been a sort of musical chairs, designed to ensure that each former company obtained a fair crack of the whip. The Southern having provided the Chairman, the others were entitled to share the remaining posts, apart from that of Deputy Chairman.

The Executive's Deputy Chairman was very different from Missenden. General Sir William (soon to become Field-Marshal Lord) Slim modestly disclaimed any special knowledge of railway management, but he obtained a great personal success with his colleagues and subordinates through his splendid, friendly personality and his quick grasp of the essentials relating to any problem brought before him. He was assigned something of a rag-bag of functions — stores, estate and rating, police, public relations and publicity — but he directed them all skilfully, delegating effectively to chief officers who were delighted to work under him. It was a matter of general regret when he resigned after only ten months, following his appointment as Chief of the Imperial General Staff. (His successor was another general, Sir Daril Watson, who was a soldier-administrator, courteous, quiet and painstaking but, not surprisingly, lacking the charisma of his famous predecessor.)

Railway operating was placed under V.M. (later Sir Michael) Barrington-Ward, Divisional General Manager (Southern Area) of the LNER. B-W, as he was universally known, was tall, with very blue eyes and a rather austere, clean-shaven face. He was a member of a distinguished family, his brothers including an editor of *The Times* and a famous surgeon. His early training had been on the Midland Railway under that wayward genius (Sir) Cecil Paget who, as General Superintendent, had, with J.H. Follows, introduced the pioneer system of train control, later extended to the whole LMS. B-W had transferred to the LNER where his fondness for Midland practices led him into a prolonged tussle with C.M. Jenkin Jones, the supreme exponent of the alternative North Eastern Railway control principles.

B-W was famous for his taciturnity. He seldom gave reasons for his decisions, but always commanded respect even from those who disagreed with him. And if a decision was taken over his head with which he disagreed, he would still loyally carry it out. His loyalty to the Midland Railway was legendary; Jenkin Jones once wrote of B-W 'putting on his Derby hat and, facing the North West, saying his morning prayers' to the gods of the Midland Pantheon.

The Commercial Member of the Executive could hardly have been more different in temperament, though physically the difference was slight, since David Blee was also slim and clean-shaven. He had been Chief Goods Manager of the Great Western, a post to which his rise had been rapid. He was a man of great sincerity and inner kindliness, but his ambition and a certain lack of humour made it difficult for him to relax. He saw himself as a super-salesman of railways and liked to relate how, when in his younger days, he had been Goods Agent at Slough, he had been accustomed after office hours to walk down to the Great West Road to watch the lorries passing and to consider each one an insult and a personal challenge. Lacking the downright approach of some of his colleagues, he was still not an intellectual like C.K. Bird or Jenkin Jones of the LNER or Wood of the LMS.

It was perhaps not surprising that David Blee built up his supporting team very largely from his old company. Great Western influence in commercial matters was looked at with some doubts by those from other companies, however, because that railway had adhered to the old-fashioned system of leaving passenger commercial matters under a Superintendent of the Line primarily concerned with operating.

The LMS scored heavily in mechanical and electrical engineering, the Member for which was Robert A. ('Robin') Riddles, who had risen to be a Vice-President of the LMS. Handsome and well-dressed, and a first-rate technical officer, he was first and foremost a steam locomotive man; he had no use for main line diesel traction as a half-way house to electrification, which he saw as the ultimate solution, though for the time being it must be postponed. It was a strongly LMS-dominated department that RAR set up and almost at once set to work on the task of designing BR standard steam locomotives, probably the most criticised action that the Executive undertook during its lifetime. He could exercise considerable charm, and expounded his arguments forcefully. However he had too lively a temperament to be able completely to conceal his irritation at meetings between the Executive and the British Transport Commission, when he was asked to explain or defend his policies by men whose professional knowledge fell short of his own. He was always at odds with Oliver Bulleid, the brilliant but unconventional CME of the Southern.

Civil engineering was placed under J.C.L. (Sir Landale) Train, who had been Chief Engineer of the LNER. Train was a tall craggy Scot who could look very distinguished in full Highland dress on festive occasions. He could be abrupt, though rather less taciturn than B-W, but anyone who took him for just a rough-neck engineer would have been sadly mistaken. Despite the furious opposition of the Divisional General Managers of the LNER, he had managed to bring all civil engineering on that line under his control instead of being decentralised under the DGM. He was, in short, a skilful politician and adept at surviving crises. Almost alone among the Executive Members he insisted on frequent inspections, usually by officer's saloon, and cultivated good relations with the BTC and also the Chief Regional Officers whom most of his colleagues tended to by-pass wherever possible. This served him in good stead eventually, leading to his becoming a Member of the British Transport Commission on the abolition of the Railway Executive, while some of his less politically adept colleagues suffered downgrading to chief officer status or were retired earlier than was absolutely necessary.

Oddly enough, Missenden took — it was said — a dislike to him. Certainly at Executive meetings, while the Chairman would address the others as 'David' or 'Robin', the Civil Engineering Member was always 'Mr Train'.

Staff matters, perhaps inevitably, were entrusted to an ex-trade-unionist. W.P. ('Bill') Allen, former General Secretary of the Associated Society of Locomotive Engineers and Firemen, was short and cheerful, with a fine old-fashioned waxed moustache. His approach was friendly and down-to-earth, and he made the move from one side of the negotiating table to the other appear quite effortless. He was not in the least inclined to try to pay off old scores, and showed a warmer personality than his counterpart in the British Transport

Commission, John Benstead from the NUR, even though he may have lacked Benstead's intellectual powers. His real success was shown by the fact that he had no enemies on either side of the negotiating table. A faintly malicious yet quite affectionate story was told about Bill Allen, derived from his dislike of formality and his insistence upon using christian names. When he was momentarily unable to remember the name of someone whom he might be clapping on the shoulder, he always fell back on 'Arthur', so that a number of pseudo-Arthurs were always around in the dusty corridors of No 222.

Of the two part-time members, Sir Wilfred Ayre and Mr C. Nevile, it must be said that the Executive did not involve them very closely in its managerial work. Sir Wilfred had a particular interest in Scottish affairs, in much the same way as some directors of pre-nationalisation companies had brought special experience of this kind to the Board table. Mr Nevile had, equally, experience in the agricultural industry to contribute.

This then was the team faced with the task of running British Railways as one business — 641,000 staff, 20,000 steam locomotives, 1,223,000 wagons, 56,000 'coaching' vehicles, and no less than 19,600 miles of route representing 52,200 miles of track. A huge undertaking indeed!

A factor which increasingly affected morale in the Regions was the way in which Executive Members directed the Regional departmental officers who for the most part were simply company officers continuing in their former positions, much to their dissatisfaction; many felt their downgrading keenly. Just a few experienced some expansion of their territorial responsibilities; for instance, the LNER Southern Area, now Eastern Region, took in from the LMS the London Tilbury & Southend line; others saw a contraction.

But each Region needed a spokesman and figure-head, and this was supposed to be provided by the appointment of Chief Regional Officers. There was, deliberately, no question of Regional General Management, but the CRO were selected from people of great ability and seniority. The Eastern Region was entrusted to C.K. Bird, an LNER man whose intellectual qualities (he had been a Wrangler at Cambridge) were outstanding. He had a quick wit and on occasion a biting tongue. The impression he gave was that the ordinary office tasks of a manager scarcely extended his brain sufficiently and could bore him. Sadly, the signs of poor health which were to lead to his death in 1958, at the age of barely 60, were already beginning to appear.

The largest Region, the London Midland, had as CRO the last (acting) President of the LMS, G.L. Darbyshire, whose expertise lay mainly in labour and establishment matters, where the LMS had a larger and perhaps more bureaucratic organisation than any other of the four main lines. His term was not long, since he retired in February 1951. As a CRO he supported his colleagues well, but at this time Euston needed a stronger hand at the helm.

The surprise appointment was in the North Eastern Region, where Charles Hopkins became the youngest CRO. He was one of the LNER's 'bright young men', his last post there being Assistant General Manager (Traffic and Statistics). The creation of a North Eastern Region had hung in the balance, the original idea being that all of the LNER in England would form one Region. There was rejoicing in York when 'NER' once more became meaningful initials.

The Scottish Region was entrusted to T.F. Cameron who had been General Manager of the Scottish Area of the LNER. His LMS counterpart was due for retirement in any case; and TFC was certainly one of the ablest men in the railway service though this did not always appear in his rather lugubrious assessment of situations. His achievement in welding together the ex-LMS and ex-LNER components in the new Region testified to his capacity, though some amusement was caused by his insistence upon continuing to occupy a flat in the North British Hotel, Edinburgh, and travelling daily (by car) to his new Regional Headquarters in Glasgow.

For the Southern Region it was inevitable that the new CRO should be John Elliot, who had identified himself with the Southern so closely ever since he had arrived in 1925 from Fleet Street to initiate a public relations organisation, rising (under Sir Herbert Walker's guiding hand) to Assistant Traffic Manager, to Deputy General Manager and, after Missenden was designated as shadow Chairman of the RE, acting General Manager of the Southern. Lively, witty, a man of the world as well as a dedicated railwayman, he nevertheless in 1948 did not yet appear the obvious heir-apparent to the Chairmanship, which he reached (via the LM Region) in 1951.

Last (alphabetically but not otherwise), the Western Region was happy to have K.W.C. Grand as CRO, whose broad grasp of railway commerical matters and cosmopolitan business outlook had been developed by his stay in New York as the railway's representative for North America. On his return to Paddington he had developed a great interest in the railway's venture into air transport, especially through Railway Air Services Ltd.

What of that — to most railwaymen — shadowy body supposed to be sitting on top of the Executive, namely the British Transport Commission? Sir Cyril Hurcomb, its Chairman, was reputed to be one of the ablest civil servants of his generation. After a long period as Permanent Secretary of the Ministry of Transport he had become Chairman of the Central Electricity Board. He returned during the war to the key position of Director-General of the Ministry of Shipping and then DG of the Ministry of War Transport which embraced both shipping and inland transport. After the war he turned to planning the nationalisation of transport, as required by the Attlee Government that had come to power in 1945.

Able Hurcomb undoubtedly was, in fact the intellectual superior of all his colleagues, but (as I wrote in an obituary notice in *The Times*), he 'had been denied by his political masters, wishful of keeping patronage in their own hands, the right to hire and fire the Members of the Executives who, under the Transport Act, were intended to carry out the policy of the BTC .... he was baffled by the obstinate independence shown by, at least, the Railway Executive'.

This independence was to manifest itself, to Hurcomb's irritation, almost at once.

Hurcomb was 64 when he took up this new and daunting responsibility, but he certainly retained his energy and indeed his impatience. Two of his colleagues on the Commission, however, were only shadows of their former selves. Lord Ashfield, the founding father of London Transport, was 73 and only ten months after the Commission came into existence he died. Sir William Wood found the change from being the executive head of the largest railway company uncongenial and he did not, at the age of 64, relish the role of planner without executive authority that Members of the Commission had perforce to accept.

Lord Rusholme, aged 57, had been, as Robert Palmer, General Secretary of the Co-operative Union Ltd. He was a capable Mancunian, practical and affable by nature, but with no special knowledge of transport. The obligatory trade union member was in years the baby of the Commission, John Benstead, aged 50, former General Secretary of the National Union of Railwaymen. Benstead was a man of great ability, and trusted by Hurcomb, who soon promoted him to be Deputy Chairman. Changing sides had not been easy for JB; he lacked the natural warmth of Bill Allen and real popularity eluded him although he always commanded the respect of those who worked directly under him.

The team was soon enlarged to include as a part-time Member Captain Sir Ian Bolton, a distinguished Scottish accountant and former Director of the LMS in Scotland. Sir Ian provided an important link between the BTC in London and the whole of their undertaking north of the Border.

Who was really in charge of the railways, the Executive or the Commission? It was too simple to say that the Executive had the duties of the former General Managers, and the Commission those of the former Boards of Directors. The Commission had been given quite complex duties including the preparation of charges schemes, which the former Boards would never have undertaken. And the Commission was a full-time body, unlike the Boards which normally only met once a month. So clashes and power struggles were inevitable between Commission and Executive, nor were they long in appearing.

Chapter 3
Lobster Quadrille

When the Labour Chancellor of the Exchequer, Dr Hugh Dalton (of whom an unkind colleague once said that his eyes 'blazed with insincerity'), made his celebrated remark about the nation having purchased a very poor bag of assets, he was referring, he explained, to the run-down condition of railway stations, permanent way and rolling stock. The observation was unfair, since the dilapidation, such as it was, had mainly arisen from over-use and under-maintenance during the war and Government restrictions on investment thereafter. It was certainly untrue, when one looked at the items in the 'bag of assets' beside the railway proper, which the nation had acquired by the compulsory purchase of the Companies' shares.

The four great railways had really been transport conglomerates. Unlike the railways in most other countries, they had invested very considerable sums in what they usually termed 'ancillary businesses'. These included workshops for manufacture as well as repair of locomotives, carriages and wagons; fleets of road vehicles for goods collection and delivery; hotels; refreshment rooms and train catering; shipping services; ports and harbours; and canals.

There were also substantial investments in bus companies, (BET Group, Tilling Group and Scottish Motor Traction Group); road haulage (Carter Paterson Ltd, Pickfords Ltd, and numerous other cartage and haulage businesses); travel agencies (Thos Cook & Son Ltd, and Dean & Dawson Ltd); airlines (British & Foreign Aviation Ltd, Railway Air Services Ltd, Channel Island Airways Ltd); and the Pullman Car Company Ltd.

This list is by no means complete; there were various other

investments and activities apart from the railway, eg property development and letting of sites for commercial advertising.

As the Transport Act was designed to lead to an 'integrated' system of public inland transport, clearly the nucleus of this system was already provided by the railways. In a last-minute attempt to produce an alternative to nationalisation that could be acceptable to the Government, Sir James Milne of the GWR had told a committee of Assistants (of which I was one) to outline proposals for turning the 'railways' into 'transport companies' The Great Western Transport Company, for instance, would have become a Regional transport authority.

The idea of letting the railways dominate such an organisation was anathema to the civil servants in the Ministry of Transport. It would have been bitterly contested by the road transport interests. It would also have been politically difficult to 'sell' to Labour MPs, except for those sponsored by the railway trade unions. It was never therefore seriously considered by the Government.

Nevertheless, the railways were going to bring valuable non-railway assets into the huge BTC conglomerate and, since Executives based on modes of transport had been decided upon, these assets had to be redistributed. This, to the civil servants and indeed to the BTC, intent upon discharging its statutory obligations, was a necessary tidying-up operation. To the Railway Executive, much of it seemed a pointless reshuffle to no particular purpose, other than a purely doctrinaire reorganisation — a lobster quadrille, in fact.

The separation from the railway proper of the 'ancillary' functions was partly due to a feeling among civil servants that the railway managements under company ownership had spread their interests too wide, distracting them from the prime task of running the railway effectively. It was also 'untidy' that railways should run buses, lorries (and perhaps even ships); and tidiness is much valued by administrators if rather less so by managers.

Tidying-up began immediately upon the passing of the

Act. The Docks and Inland Waterways Executive took over the railway-owned canals easily; the railways were glad to see them go! The railway-owned docks and ports were more of a problem; some were classified as 'packet ports', mainly used by railway steamer services, to remain with the Railway Executive; others like Hull and the ex-GWR South Wales ports, were 'trade harbours', to go to the DIWE.

The transfer of the docks went fairly smoothly for a time. King's Lynn docks passed to the DIWE in July 1948; the South Wales ports, formerly managed by the GWR, in August, and the ex-LNER docks at Hull, Grimsby and Immingham at the end of the year.

But Missenden had been a former Docks and Marine Manager of the Southern Railway. And Southampton, with its modern Ocean Terminal, had been one of the achievements and most prized possessions of that company. He led the objections of the Executive to the transfer on the grounds that it was basically a packet port — Ocean Terminal and all — and as such it should remain with the railways.

Hurcomb disliked over-ruling the Executives, preferring to let agreement emerge. So the Southampton transfer correspondence went on for some time, but in the end the Commission, urged on by Sir Robert Letch, the forceful (though blind) Deputy Chairman of the Docks Executive, finally insisted on the transfer which took place in September 1950.

Another transfer had to be accepted, as there was statutory· provision for it, the Act having included the creation 'on a date to be appointed' of an Hotels Executive, to which not merely the hotels but the refreshment rooms and restaurant car services would be transferred. This Executive was set up on 1 April 1948, under the chairmanship of the very appropriately-named Lord Inman.

For the time being there was no move to segregate the workshops, the shipping services or the road collection and delivery fleets. But the Commission took over direct control of the investments in road transport and travel agencies. The Road Transport Executive, originally apparently expected to cover. both passenger and freight services, was soon (from June 1949) split into two, namely a Road Haulage Executive and a Road Passenger Executive. The railway investments in road carriers and hauliers were transferred to the RHE and formed the nucleus of the huge undertaking which was to become British Road Services through the compulsory acquisition of long-distance road haulage businesses under the Act.

But the bus company investments were not transferred to the Road Passenger Executive, which was created in order to plan a future organisation based upon area schemes embracing all road passenger services in each area, an ambitious concept that never came to fruition. Instead, the Commission allowed the railway liaison with the BET bus companies, in which the four main line Companies had had shareholdings, to continue. The other two main bus groups, Tilling and Scottish Motor Traction, were nationalised by an agreed purchase by the BTC of the non-railway-owned shares, the Tilling companies in November 1948 and the SMT Group in March 1949, thus giving the Commission full control, although the company structure was allowed to continue virtually unchanged.

The railway investment in air transport was brought to a rapid end, despite the recommendation of the wartime Cadman Committee that the railways should after the war be allowed to continue to develop internal air services as they had been doing before the war. The Attlee Government was nationalising everything it could, so putting the new state corporations into neat spheres of activity. They were not allowed to overlap even if this might have commercial advantages; this was anathema to tidy-minded Whitehall.

So this quadrille of changing partners was performed; it was a rather ominous precursor of the series of reorganisations that were to plague the railways throughout their first 25 years after nationalisation, constantly diverting management away from the real tasks demanding attention.

Chapter 4
Early Problems and Achievements

When the Railway Executive assumed control of the railways, the winter was not very far advanced. As matters were to turn out, it was to be a mild one. But no one, least of all the Government, yet was sûre that the country was not going to experience a repetition of those cruel months of January, February and March 1947, when snow lay almost continuously on the ground. Everyone shivered from electricity cuts, reduced gas pressures and acute shortages of all solid fuels, and many people had to go to bed in dark unheated rooms; all transport was carried on with difficulty and at times it seemed as though spring would never come.

The following summer was very hot. But the Government felt disinclined to take a chance on a mild winter and it set up a Winter Transport Executive Committee, chaired by a future Prime Minister, Mr L.J. Callaghan, MP, who was then Parliamentary Secretary to the Ministry of Transport. Sir Cyril Hurcomb sat on this Committee, and acted as liaison between it and the Railway Executive.

The Committee helped the railways in some respects, for instance by giving priority for materials required for locomotive and wagon repairs, and launching a campaign to persuade traders to co-operate in securing a rapid turnround of railway wagons.

In another way, though, the Committee took a panic measure, not altogether dissimilar to the ill-judged coal/oil conversions for locomotives in 1946-47, which in the long term adversely affected the railways. It had arranged in the autumn of 1947 to divert quite a lot of rail traffic away to road, either to haulage firms or to the use of traders' own vehicles. Then, ironically, the winter turned out to be mild and the diversions were quite unnecessary. But the special measures were not cancelled until March 1948, and by then the railways had lost a lot of traffic, much of it permanently, to road.

Just three months before nationalisation, the four main line railways, through the Railway Executive Committee that had been the instrument of Government control during the war and immediate post-war period, had put to the Minister of Transport a five-year plan for construction and repair of rolling stock. In it they assumed that 35 years was the normal life of railway locomotives, wagons and carriages. By this test 39.3 per cent of the locomotives, 27.8 per cent of all wagons, and 23.6 per cent of passenger carriages were over-age. They wished to build 574 locomotives in 1948 and an average of 782 annually for the next four years thereafter.

Some locomotives were in fact as much as 70 years old; many passenger carriages were between 40 and 50 years old. The wagon position was rather better, as substantial numbers had been built during the war.

The Government had pigeon-holed the report, in view of impending nationalisation. In the background was the Government's attempt rigidly to control investment at home, largely in the interests of stimulating exports. In the White Paper 'Capital Investment in 1948' it was stated that 'the Government think that during 1948 supplies of materials for permanent way must, because of the steel shortage, be reduced to current needs, about the same as pre-war, but without overtaking arrears'.

The new Railway Executive looked hard at the situation it had inherited. It pointed out the substantial handicaps upon operation, including the large number of permanent speed restrictions due to the condition of the track and also many bridges, or imposed temporarily during essential repair or renewal work. Then there was the poor quality of much locomotive coal, leading to loss of steam pressure and failures in traffic.

The Executive put in several reports on the position to its nominal overlord, the British Transport Commission. The first of these was prepared as early as March 1948; it was entitled 'The Physical Condition of British Railways, January 1948'. It pointed out that the cost of arrears of maintenance, abnormal wear and tear and war damage amounted to £179 millions. In spite of this, current traffics were 30 per cent over the pre-war level for passengers and 20 per cent for freight.

The Executive proposed (a) 'to take the actual assets acquired at 1 January 1948, and to consider how far they will meet the requirements in 1948 and later under conditions of railway unification, and if not the extent of the deficiences and the remedies requiring action; (b) to concentrate future policy on reducing costs and increasing the efficiency of the plant and equipment; (c) to develop a commercial policy which will attract the maximum passenger and freight traffic that can be carried'.

A review of the locomotive position concluded that the total stock was adequate, but the number under and awaiting repair urgently needed to be reduced. But the stock of passenger carriages was inadequate; it was 2,609 vehicles less than in December 1939 though traffic was 30 per cent greater. The wagon position was dealt with separately in a special report containing a proposal described later.

Much stress was laid on the need quickly to restore the condition of the permanent way and structures. The Commission was warned that the railways were in urgent need of finance and steel allocations to bring up the physical condition to an acceptable level.

Despite all these handicaps, the Executive was able to achieve improved train performance in 1948 compared with the last year before nationalisation. The improvement in punctuality was of course largely due to the fact that 1948 had seen no repetition of the appalling winter weather conditions and the fuel crisis of the first quarter of 1947. But in other ways also, post-war improvements were taking effect. The 1948 summer timetables showed a booked weekly train mileage of 248,000 miles more than in the previous year. Named trains were on the increase; The Queen of Scots Pullman was restored between London and Glasgow via Leeds and Harrogate; a new Great Central line express from Marylebone to Bradford was introduced named The South Yorkshireman; and The Flying Scotsman, with new partly air-conditioned stock, again ran non-stop between London and Edinburgh. The Southern Region instituted a new Pullman train between London and Ramsgate called The Thanet Belle.

The punctuality figures would have shown an even greater improvement had it not been for an unexpectedly cruel trick played by nature in the summer of 1948. Six days of heavy and almost continuous rain in early August swelled the rivers and caused extensive flooding in the Scottish Border country, to such an extent that bridges and embankments were washed away on the East Coast main line, especially between Berwick and Burnmouth. The Waverley route from Carlisle to Edinburgh and the Tweedmouth-St Boswells and Reston — St Boswells lines were also damaged, so that by 12/13 August *all* the former LNER lines between England and Scotland were out of action. Between Reston and Grantshouse no less than seven bridges were washed away. At one point hundreds of tons of debris were deposited on the track.

After a short time it became possible to operate passenger services over the less seriously damaged sections via Tweedmouth, St Boswells and thence by the Waverley route to Edinburgh, all freight being diverted via Carlisle. The restoration of the East Coast Main Line however was a major task in which, as the Executive recorded 'experts in temporary bridge construction from the Regions and from the Royal Engineers were sent to advise on the problem; large quantities of material were assembled at suitable points; contractors were quickly on the scene with a large assortment of mechanical plant, including excavators, bulldozers and cranes; emergency pumping equipment was loaned by the Metropolitan Water Board; and 22 mobile coaches were used to feed and house 545 men specially drafted to the area'.

This huge effort enabled the line to be re-opened for freight traffic on 25 October and for passenger traffic a week later.

The replacement of the temporary bridges was of course a longer task, but was put in hand as soon as possible.

At this time I was Assistant Secretary (Works and Development) of the BTC and, both in this capacity and as a former LNER officer, was intensely interested in this unique operation. I visited the scene of the flood disasters, escorted by W.Y. Sandeman, the energetic Civil Engineer of the Scottish Region, a former LNER colleague. I was amazed at the extent of the damage. Over the Eye Water, for instance, between Berwick and Dunbar, well over 200ft of embankment and bridge had completely collapsed. The temporary wooden trestle that was being erected hastily to reopen the line reminded one of the pictures of early American railroad bridges; despite involving a severe speed restriction it served its purpose admirably until the embankment and a permanent new bridge could replace it.

Apart from this calamity, day-to-day traffic problems were less than might have been anticipated, and the Executive early on started to seek its declared objective of obtaining the maximum benefit from the unification of British Railways. The Executive claimed — something which later critics have doubted — that it was not just seeking to make good the arrears of maintenance that had accumulated during and since the war (in other words, to get back to pre-war standards) but trying 'to measure the existing assets against the requirements of 1948 and later years under conditions of transport unification'.

The intentions were clearly good; what (with hindsight) now seems to have been lacking was a realistic appraisal of long-term traffic prospects and the future strength of road competition.

Looking ahead, the Executive at the end of 1948 had prepared a report entitled 'Major Development Schemes: Five Years 1948 to 1952'. In it were listed the major works authorised by the boards of the former companies, together with some £2.5 million of expenditure on works costing over £100,000 each, subsequently authorised by the Executive. It then set out some £48 million worth of works which it calculated could be started in the five-year period, and £55 million worth of 'other works which would have been considered had resources been available'.

The most important of the works in hand that had been authorised and started by the companies were to be found on the LNER and were the belated fruits of the 1935-40 New Works Programme; they included the Manchester-Sheffield-Wath electrification (the first true main line electrification in Britain using locomotives for both passenger and freight trains); the associated new Woodhead Tunnel; and the electrification from Liverpool Street to Shenfield. The Southern Railway Board had approved in principle the elimination of steam traction from all its lines east of the Reading/Portsmouth axis, through electrification of the more important routes and the introduction of diesel traction on the minor lines and branches.

The Executive declared its intention of completing the works that had already been started, but taking a fresh look at those authorised but not started, as well as others at various stages of planning in the New Works departments. Some of those that were shelved were of great importance. The Southern Railway plans were put into abeyance for the time being. And the scheme that had been approved in outline by the Board of the LNER, for full conversion of the East Coast Main Line express passenger services to diesel traction, through the purchase of 25 large diesel-electric locomotives, was not merely shelved but consigned to the waste-paper basket. This was a serious mistake. The experience gained from such a move into main line diesel traction would have been invaluable when funds for modernisation on a large scale became available.

The Commission did not feel able to challenge the Executive's decision in this case. But soon another issue arose on which the Commission found itself rather concerned at what was proposed. The Executive had created an 'Ideal Stocks' Committee to determine the future size and character of the wagon fleet. The Committee compared the existing fleet with what it estimated would be the fleet required to handle the traffics of 1950. Surprisingly, it showed a surplus of coal wagons amounting to 115,420, against a deficiency in open merchandise wagons of 30,470. After a proposed re-allocation of suitable coal wagons to merchandise traffic, there was a surplus of 84,950 coal wagons which the Railway Executive told the Commission should be broken up without replacement.

I was present at the meeting between the Commission and the Executive at which the latter body outlined this rather drastic proposal. Sir Cyril Hurcomb's initial reaction was one of pained surprise. He pointed out that if these wagons were, as he understood, former private owners' wagons, they had, under the Transport Act, just been compulsorily purchased by the BTC. Had all that money, certainly running into seven figures, been thrown away in buying worthless and unneeded rolling stock?

The Executive replied that unified ownership should improve turn-rounds compared with pre-war conditions, and that the wagons to be broken up would be at least 37 years old, in poor condition, and mostly grease-lubricated instead of oil-lubricated. Eliminating them would have operating advantages and reduce repair costs. Grease boxes meant that the wagons ran less freely, especially in cold weather, than those fitted with oil axleboxes. More hot boxes occurred with grease, and in hump yards, especially, it was a handicap that wagons with oil lubrication ran faster and tended to overtake grease-box wagons so that proper sorting might be impossible.

The Commission was only half convinced. Had the point been put sooner to the Government, the unwanted grease-box wagons might have been left out of the purchase altogether. So much money down the drain, so soon after nationalisation, brought some distrust of the Executive's planning; it was to be followed by other instances. Probably the underlying cause was the placing of ultimate financial reponsibility upon the Commission, but entrusting management to a separate Executive, not effectively controlled by the Commission, whose actions nevertheless determined the financial out-turn of the business as a whole.

The case of the wagons bought in order to be scrapped was soon followed by the announcement of a steam locomotive building policy which, again, the Commission felt unable to insist should be changed, but about which it had serious doubts.

Chapter 5
Steam Tactics

Readers of Rudyard Kipling will remember that the title above is that of a short story about the adventures of a steam motor car putting up a gallant but ineffective struggle to survive in an age when the internal combustion engine was relentlessly taking over. Echoes of this situation are to be found in the years from 1948 to 1955 on British Railways.

The Railway Executive inherited from the companies 20,023 steam locomotives of 448 types. It also of course inherited building programmes that had acquired momentum — materials on order, workshop time and space allocations, as well as orders placed with contractors — which for the most part were allowed to continue. In the first year after national-isation, 299 steam locomotives were built in railway shops, 96 were purchased new from contractors and 558 WD freight locomotives were bought from the Ministry of Supply second-hand: they had already been at work on BR; 14 diesel shunters and one electric locomotive completed the picture.

But the Executive had also inherited from the companies a small fleet of diesel locomotives. There were 53 diesel-electrics, mostly of the 0-6-0 shunter type and chiefly from the LMS, which had proved reliable and economical. But there were also the two 1,600 hp English Electric LMS main line proto-types. In the pipeline, ordered before nationalisation, were two 1,600hp diesel-electric locomotives for the Southern, one 1,600hp diesel-mechanical locomotive on the 'Fell' principle for the LMS, two gas-turbine locomotives for the Great Western, and an 827hp diesel-electric, ordered by the LMS for secondary services.

The first real intimation of the Executive's approach to traction policy came when the Commission learnt that,

although the locomotive testing station at Rugby, commissioned jointly by the LMS and the LNER, was approaching
completion (it was opened on 19 October 1948), the Executive
intended to carry out a very extensive programme of locomotive exchanges to measure the comparative performance
of some of the principal company designs. The tests would
include express passenger, general-purpose and freight
locomotives and would extend from mid-April until September
1948.

While this was obviously going to provide enormous interest
for railway buffs and rich material for railway photographers,
it did not seem relevant to the prime question which nearly all
major railways in the world were asking themselves — what
was to be the future role of steam, diesel and electric traction
in the post-war world?

My deputy, a splendid Yorkshireman named Leslie Marson,
and I discussed the position and agreed that it would now be
appropriate if the Commission were to ask the Executive
exactly what its attitude was to the longer-term issues of
traction policy. I drafted a letter suggesting that a good deal of
technical information had accumulated on the newer forms of
traction, but that it seemed urgent to study the estimated
future economic balance between steam, diesel and electric
power. The Chief Secretary agreed and placed the letter
before Sir Cyril Hurcomb who signed it. It remained un-
answered for eight months.

Meanwhile the RE trials went merrily on. The express
passenger locomotives included an ex-LMS Duchess 4-6-2, a
Gresley streamlined A4 4-6-2, a Southern Merchant Navy
4-6-2, with an ex-GWR King 4-6-0 and an ex-LMS rebuilt
Royal Scot 4-6-0. The routes on which the trials took place
were King's Cross-Leeds, Euston-Carlisle, Paddington-
Plymouth and Waterloo-Exeter. These tests were supplemented by those of four general-purpose locomotive types, a
Southern West Country 4-6-2 and three 4-6-0 types, the ex-
LMS Class 5, Thompson ex-LNER B1 and a WR Hall. The
routes here included the Highland main line from Perth to

Inverness, the Midland line from St Pancras to Manchester and the Great Central line from Marylebone to Manchester.

The trials have provided a considerable literature and were interesting and indeed enjoyable to many people. Whether in fact they served any particular purpose is doubtful, since Riddles and his team at 222 Marylebone Road had already decided to design a range of new standard steam locomotives; in the first Annual Report, that for 1948, it was recorded by the Executive that 'preliminary designs were prepared in consultation with the operating department and are being examined by the Civil Engineers regarding route availability and clearances'. There was thus no idea of using the exchange trials for the purpose of selecting one or more company designs for perpetuation on British Railways. Their purpose was perhaps psychological rather than technical, to persuade Motive Power Superintendents that types other than those locomotives with which they were familiar could perform satisfactorily, and thus help to break down any prejudice against new BR standard designs when these should appear.

Cecil J. Allen, who described the trials at length in his book *The Locomotive Exchanges*, has pointed out how their validity was affected by the fact that there was no common standard of driving. (This of course has long been a characteristic of British locomotive practice, and one that surprises foreign railwaymen, the latitude allowed to drivers in the way they handle their engines, contrasting strongly with the strict control exercised over, for instance, French drivers.)

Equally detrimental to proper comparison was the lack of uniformity in the 'conducting' which was provided by the 'home' Region, and required because each locomotive was handled by a driver who was familiar with it, but not with the 'foreign' route chosen for the test. Allen added that 'some drivers were barely attempting to keep time, or were losing time by the slackest of uphill running, so as to pinch coal consumption to the minimum in the hope of regaining the lost minutes by unduly fast running down the next favourable stretch'. This underlines the point that if the trials had been intended to compare performance under completely controlled conditions, excluding the effects of weather, of signal delays and changing speed restrictions, for instance, one would have thought that the Rugby testing station would have yielded more reliable data. It could perhaps plausibly be argued that both types of test were needed.

Another enjoyable exercise was embarked upon when, less than a month after nationalisation, the Railway Executive held the first of several 'beauty contests' to decide upon the future livery for BR locomotives and coaching stock. On 30 January 1948 at Kensington (Olympia) on the West London line, a selection of ex-LMS 4-6-0 locomotives paraded in GWR green, LNER green and Southern Malachite green, with a dramatic final appearance of a 4-6-0 in LNWR black that stole the scene. In addition, there was a Southern Region electric locomotive finished in light blue.

There were also some examples of coaching stock, one in a variation of the GWR chocolate and cream, a red which was some way off true Midland crimson lake, together with an electric multiple-unit set in Southern green.

This led to no firm conclusion other than to apply the GWR green to express passenger locomotives. A further exhibition was then arranged at Marylebone station. More adventurous liveries were on show and it was announced that they would be standardised in future. Royal blue with black and white lining was to be used for heavy duty express passenger engines, green with black and orange lining would be applied to other passenger engines, while all other types were to be in black.

Even this decision was not permanent. By the summer of 1948 14 trains in experimental liveries were placed in service on selected main line and cross-country routes, as a public relations exercise; the public were invited to send their comments on the liveries to the Executive.

The trial colours were:

For the most powerful express passenger locomotives:
    Blue, with lining of red, cream and grey.

A

B

C

Portraits of Chairmen
RE/BTC/BRB

A Sir Eustace Missenden
(1948–51) with the locomotive
named after him. (*British Rail*)
B (Sir) John Elliot (1951–53).
(*British Rail*)
C Sir Brian (Lord) Robertson
(1953–61). (*BBC/Hulton Picture
Library*)
D Dr (Lord) Beeching
(1961–65). (*British Rail*)
E (Sir) Stanley Raymond
(1965–67). (*British Rail*)
F (Sir) Henry Johnson
(1967–71). (*British Rail*)
G (Sir) Richard Marsh
(1971–76). (*British Rail*)

D

E

F

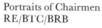

G

A

B

C

D

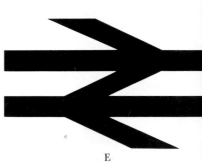

E

Signs and totems!
A The first 'Wembley lion' emblem. (*British Rail*)
B The improved 'heraldic' lion of 1956. (*Crown copyright National Railway Museum*)
C What *might* have adorned locomotives – the full grant of arms to the BTC! (*British Rail*)
D The 'flying sausages' sign. (*David & Charles*)
E The double-arrow of the 1960s. (*British Rail*)

Other express passenger locomotives: Green with lining
of red, cream and grey.
Mixed traffic locomotives: Black with lining of red, grey
and cream (virtually LNWR livery).
Freight locomotives: Black.
Main-line corridor trains: (a) Plum and spilt milk, lined
with bands of yellow-maroon-yellow separated by lines
of spilt milk (b) Chocolate and cream lined with black
and golden yellow.
Local suburban trains: Maroon, lined with golden
yellow-black-golden yellow.
Multiple-unit electric trains: Green.
The blue livery looked well — surprisingly — on a GWR
King. But, somehow, Great Western green looked almost
dingy when applied to a LMS Stanier Jubilee 4-6-0, lacking
the copper and brass embellishments with which Swindon
emphasized the basic colour. And Riddles' attempt to recreate
the LNWR blackberry-black livery did not entirely succeed
on a locomotive that did not have the classic LNWR lines.

Another exercise in North-Western nostalgia failed to come
off. The plum and spilt milk was disappointingly unlike the
real LNWR livery; it was perhaps closer to that of the
Caledonian, in which there *was* something of plum colour in
the lower panels. In any case, it lost a great deal from the
absence of the elaborate mouldings and the lining of the
upper panels that had given character to pre-grouping LNWR
and CR stock. The maroon colour, too, was a sad decline from
Midland crimson lake.

After the experimental liveries had been given several
months' trial, the Executive quietly dropped the lining on
some of the black locomotives and changed the lining of green
engines to orange-black-orange. It also abandoned both the
plum and spilt milk and the chocolate and cream for coaching
stock and standardised instead on a new two-colour scheme,
officially maroon and cream, unofficially blood and custard,
in which the lower bodywork was painted in a red that was a
very long way from the Midland lake and even from the LMS

maroon. Non-corridor carriages and non-passenger-carrying coaching stock were simply painted in red overall.

The shortage of staff for cleaning locomotives and of washing machines for coaching stock made the whole exercise pretty unrealistic. The main lesson that emerged was that the liveries of the former companies had seemed to suit the designs of their locomotives and coaching stock very well, and sat uneasily on other companies' stock. Was there really any need to search for a new BR livery when most stock worked within a Region corresponding fairly closely to a former company? The moral seemed to be that the virtues of unification and standardisation could easily be exaggerated!

In its section of the BTC Report for 1948 the RE noted that an 'interesting post has been established . . . . that of Executive Officer (Design). This appointment was a necessity as it could obviously no longer be left to the Regions to produce locomotives and rolling stock as in the days before national-isation'. The use of the word 'obviously' shows that the alternatives had not been seriously considered.

The alternatives would have been to continue building those company types that were performing successfully on their home Regions, to refresh the existing stocks until a new traction policy could be developed for BR as a whole; or to select a very few for more general use, if they had wide route availability and satisfactory maintenance cost levels. The inter-Regional trials might have been designed for the latter purpose, one might have thought. But it was not so; as E.S. Cox has recorded in *Locomotive Panorama*, by June 1948 a first list of 12 standard locomotive types for future construction had already been drawn up and, with some modification, formed the basis for the controversial programme of building new standard locomotives, which started in 1951 and, when it ground to a halt in 1960, had included 999 engines. The most outstanding feature of the programme was that some of the types were needed but others were either unsatisfactory or not needed. For instance, no less than 251 were built of the successful Class 9 2-10-0, 172 of the general-purpose Class 5

4-6-0, 115 of the Class 4 4-6-0 mixed-traffic; and 155 of the 2-6-4T Class 4. But only one (unhappily under-boilered) Class 8 Pacific was ever built and that as a replacement of No 46202 *Princess Anne*, destroyed in the Harrow accident. Even the considerably more successful Britannia Class 7 4-6-2 locomotives only numbered 55. Other classes came out in small numbers which hardly justified the effort put into the design and tooling-up in the workshops that they involved.

One must therefore wonder why, if it really was worth designing new types at all at such a period in railway history, four or five classes, backed by the perpetuation of some of the most successful company designs would not have sufficed. After all, the immediate effect on the new standard designs was to add yet more types to the total to be maintained and for which spares needed to be provided.

The building of company designs and BR standard designs compares as follows, looking forward to the end of steam locomotive construction on BR:

Steam Locomotive Construction
1948-60

	Company designs	BR standard	Total
1948	395	—	395
1949	357	—	357
1950	385	—	385
1951	208	89	297
1952	114	97	211
1953	28	123	151
1954	24	184	208
1955	18	156	174
1956	9	129	138
1957	3	141	144
1958	—	62	62
1959	—	15	15
1960	—	3	3
Total	1541	999	2540

Of course it will immediately be noted that in total since nationalisation, more company designed locomotives (some extensively modified from their original design) were built than BR standard types. One obviously must wonder whether the effort devoted to the latter was worth while.

During the months in 1948 when the locomotive interchanges were taking place, the experimental liveries were being tried out, and the first plans for building new standard locomotives were being made, the Commission's request for a report on traction policy received no answer until December 1948, when the Executive reported that it had set up a Committee to consider the problems involved. It was to be nearly three years before the Report was produced, by which time the programme for building standard steam locomotives had acquired considerable momentum.

Looking back, one can see that this was all the result of having a 'functional' Executive, in which a specialist Member was the final authority within his own field, instead of being one of a team, led by a General Manager.

The steam locomotive policy was doubly unfortunate. It involved an immediate waste of resources which would have been better employed in obtaining the best results from the best company designs in existence, by rebuilding and improving them in ways that had already transformed the economy and the performance of several famous locomotive classes. And in the longer term, when a change to diesel traction became inevitable, there was a lack of experience which was to cost the railways dearly. Furthermore, being late off the mark led to undue haste in traction conversion, with unsuitable types of diesel being ordered without sufficient trial running. If only a steady progress into diesel and electric traction had been planned and started in 1948, coupled with limited continued building and rebuilding of the most successful company steam locomotive designs, a great deal of money would have been saved and merchants' yards such as Woodhams at Barry would not have seen so many relatively new engines awaiting their turn to be scrapped. Moreover there was a good example in France, where the changeover was less precipitate and where the steam locomotive did not suddenly become anomalous and a nuisance to maintain, as happened on BR. On this principle, steam could have been retained longer over here, and properly maintained in 'pockets' of steam traction if an earlier start and a much steadier pace had been set between say 1950 and 1970.

Chapter 6
The Executive Gets Into Its Stride

By 1950 the Railway Executive seemed to be in an entrenched position both as regards its nominal master, the Commission, and its nominal subordinates, the Regions. It was concentrating strongly upon standardisation and the economies to be obtained from unified control. With one hand, it held off the Commission from interfering, as it might be termed, with railway management; with the other, it constantly reminded the Regions that they were not the successors of the companies but simply agents for RE.

So far as integration was concerned, the Executive had little time for this, though it attended the meetings of a Standing Conference on Co-ordination, presided over by Hurcomb. This body tried to make a start upon combining road and rail services by transferring container loads from road to rail for trunk haulage, and developing road services in place of railway branch line services. Experimental schemes for road-rail co-ordination in East Anglia and the Isle of Wight were also discussed in 1949, but came to very little.

Not that the RE always came off best in a tussle with the Commission. The latter body decided to set up a common legal service for all the Executives instead of each Executive maintaining its own legal department, the relations between the new service and the managements to be that of solicitor and client. The RE objected strongly, going so far as to write to the BTC: 'If the Commission are determined to proceed with this scheme, the Railway Executive would ask that a formal direction should be issued to them as they are unwilling to let it appear that the scheme has been accepted voluntarily'. This last-ditch stand was of no avail, however.

So far as the Regions were concerned, the RE was beginning

to break down any lingering company traditions by various means. One was to change (or 'rationalise') the Regional boundaries. The London, Tilbury & Southend line had been transferred from the LM Region to the Eastern Region, and the sections of the former LMS in Central and South Wales to the Western Region. Then, from April 1950, purely geo-graphical boundaries were drawn for the Regions, further divorcing them from the company structure. Here, however, a snag developed. The Chief Regional Officers preferred a system basis to geographical areas and, in particular, objected to a proposed transfer of the LM main Birmingham-Bristol line to the Western Region and of the Great Central main line north of Aylesbury to the London Midland Region. (It must be admitted that some of those boundary changes produced rather absurd results. For instance, Marylebone station was first designated Eastern Region and fitted with blue Regional signs; then it was transferred to the Western Region, and completely re-signed in chocolate, and finally transferred to the London Midland, and re-signed in red! That was not all for more recently it has been re-signed in black and white).

Apart from the objections of the Chief Regional Officers, the operating officers made strong representations to Barring-ton-Ward that cutting across the operational responsibilities based on traffic flows would be unworkable and impracticable. B-W pressed this point strongly with his colleagues, with the result that an uneasy compromise was reached. From April 1950 there would be *two* types of Region — one a system of lines applying to the operating and motive power functions, another a geographical area, for all other purposes.

The Executive had another weapon up its sleeve for preventing the Regions from being too uppish. This was to break down old company loyalties by transferring officers between Regions, a process that was assisted by the retirement of some very senior people. Among railway potentates the Chief Mechanical Engineers had been outstandingly powerful. Now in 1949 Oliver Bulleid of the Southern, A.H. Peppercorn of the Eastern and North Eastern, and F.W. Hawksworth of the Western, all retired. The last to go was H.G. Ivatt of the London Midland, in 1951. Their disappearance caused a sigh of relief among the Riddles team at 222 Marylebone Road, and their positions were immediately downgraded, partly by appointing separate Carriage and Wagon Engineers and, in the Western Region, taking away motive power operation and placing it under a Motive Power Superintendent.

'Divide and rule' seemed a good policy to the RE. Shuffling Chief Regional Officers around was helpful; when a dyed-in-the-wool LMS man, G.L. Darbyshire, retired from Euston, John Elliot from Waterloo was moved across the replace him; the consequential moves involved bringing Charles Hopkins from York to Waterloo, and sending H.A. Short, a former Southern officer who might have expected preferment to Waterloo, to York.

Out on the line, and away from the manoeuvring and politics of headquarters, progress was continuing. The most agreeable event of 1949 was the opening in September of the Liverpool Street — Shenfield electrification, started by the LNER before the war, which at last gave the long-suffering commuters of Ilford and Gidea Park a clean, frequent and faster journey. The public response was immediate; by December, weekly journeys had increased by 58 per cent over the corresponding week in 1948.

The Southern Region was trying another method of improving its suburban services by increasing the seating capacity of its inner suburban trains with the adoption of double-decking. This ingenious design by O.V.S. Bulleid was tried out towards the end of 1949. The limitations of the British loading gauge made two full-height passenger sections impossible and a form of 'interlocking' had to be adopted.

Also in 1949, the policy of naming express trains was developed. A new non-stop train to Edinburgh was introduced, The Capitals Limited, preceding The Flying Scotsman, which continued to leave at its traditional time of 10.00 but with three stops. Novelties were the names given to trains local to the Scottish Region — The Bon Accord, The St Mungo and

The Granite City (all Glasgow-Aberdeen); The Fife Coast Express (Glasgow-St Andrews); and The Irishman (Glasgow-Stranraer). The Fenman was a title given to a Liverpool Street-Hunstanton train. In total, 38 named trains were run in 1949 in an attempt to attract passengers, and counteract a drop in traffic compared with 1947.

The Executive was also concerned about safety and had started investigation into a number of steps designed to improve standards. In 1948 it began looking at the alternative systems of automatic train control (later to be more correctly termed automatic warning systems) and by 1950 the Eastern Region main line between New Barnet and Huntingdon had been equipped experimentally with a modified form of the former LMS Hudd system. (The Hudd system, unlike the GWR mechanical contact ramp, used permanent and electro-magnetic inductors and had been tried out by the LMS on the Fenchurch Street-Southend line). Extension of track circuiting and of the so-called 'Welwyn control' was also planned. This was a form of automation using track circuits to lock and release signals and block instruments to prove that a train, once signalled, had in fact passed out of a block section, and was introduced following a collision on the LNER at Welwyn Garden City in 1935.

Sadly, accidents continued to occur on a scale that disturbed the Commission. There had been three major train accidents on the London Midland Region in 1948 (Winsford, Wath Road and Stockport) one on the Eastern Region, and one in the Scottish Region. The Commission pressed the Executive to proceed with measures for improving safety and then — so capricious is Fortune — in 1949 not a single passenger was killed in a train accident.

The fluctuating incidence of accidents and fatalities was matched by a parallel uncertainty over the policy for intro-ducing aws. On the one hand the Commission, urged on by the Ministry and the railway unions, pressed the Executive for a firm forecast — in Hurcomb's favourite phrase, known to the staff as his three Ps, 'there must be a policy, a plan and a programme'. On the other hand, the Executive emphasized the need for exhaustive trials of the new system they were developing, combining the best features of the Hudd and the former Great Western systems, and the heavy cost of equipping the whole of the main lines.

A curious and unusual incident took place, when a settlement of the roof and walls caused the closure of Arley tunnel, between Nuneaton and Birmingham. Repairs took about nine months and necessitated extensive re-routing of traffic. The Civil Engineers became anxious about the possibility of similar incidents and an informal warning was given to the management that 100 years might be about the safe life-time of brick tunnel linings, so that accelerated expenditure on tunnel repairs might have to be faced in future. Fortunately, this proved to be a rather pessimistic view (although the Penmanshiel tunnel collapse in 1979 and Falkirk tunnel subsidence in 1980 were later reminders that tunnels are *not* immortal).

By 1950 a number of the Railway Executive's projects were in hand or completed. The first designs for standard passenger carriages — later known as the BR Mark I stock — were completed. The mechanised foundry at Horwich, projected in LMS days, came into service. The celebrated 50-ton iron-ore hopper wagons, with power discharge, for the Tyne Dock-Consett run (a sort of pioneer merry-go-round service) were ordered. And, at first sight surprisingly, 9,200 coal wagons were purchased from French Railways. Actually they had been built to British standards during 1944-45, though equipped with modifications to meet Continental requirements, and had been used to help get traffic moving again after the liberation of France. The SNCF no longer required them and they required little alteration to be made suitable for running on British Railways.

By now the new standard liveries were almost universal. Blue had been abandoned for the largest express passenger locomotives, which were now painted the same green as the others. Passenger coaches were, except on Southern Region which somehow contrived to continue turning out its steam coaches in green for as long as possible, painted in the maroon-and-cream livery if they were of corridor type; non-corridor vehicles were being painted in the maroon throughout. Neither schemes suited Gresley's varnished teak stock where paint did not take well on the teak panels.

There was an extensive programme of re-signing stations with the RE's standard totem signs in Regional colours. On locomotives, a lion-and-wheel totem had replaced the plain legend BRITISH RAILWAYS on tenders or tank sides. This much-criticised 'bicycling lion' was derived from a more complex design for the BTC seal, which the Commission had asked Mr Cecil Thomas, FRBS, to prepare. This was officially described as 'a lion bestriding a composite symbol which includes a wheel; a winged arrow superimposed on a pattern of wavy lines symbolising the activities of the Docks and Inland Waterways Executive; and a pair of torches emitting flashes of lightning, symbolising modern forms of power'. The winged arrow, the waves and the lightning were then omitted from the British Railways version to produce a rather anaemic reminiscence of the 'Wembley lion' of the British Empire Exhibition of 1924.

By 1950 train services had made some progress towards returning to their pre-war standard, though there was still a great deal of leeway to be made up. In the previous year an analysis of the fastest daily times between London and 48 major provincial centres showed that in only one case (predictably, Brighton, with a standard time of 60 minutes) did journeys not take longer than in 1939. To York, 1 hour 15 minutes more was taken; to Aberdeen, 2 hours 5 minutes and to Glasgow 1 hour 50 minutes. But there was a plethora of named trains, presumably intended to cast a touch of glamour over rather uninspiring performances. It is perhaps not unfair to say that hitherto, pre-war standards were the goal, and that a fundamental re-thinking of the railways' function and prospects had not yet been undertaken. But winds of change were beginning to blow, and the Executive was soon to feel their impact.

Chapter 7
Winds of Change Begin to Blow

Early in 1951 the Minister of Transport appointed F.A. Pope, then Chairman of the Ulster Transport Authority and a former Vice-President of the LMS Railway, to be a full-time Member of the BTC. About the same time, Missenden retired from the Chairmanship of the Railway Executive and was succeeded by John Elliot, CRO of the London Midland Region. And in October of the same year the General Election led to a Conservative Government taking office, an administration which had very different views about transport and the railways in particular.

All these events, in different ways, affected the relations between the BTC and the Railway Executive and indirectly bore upon the plans and policies that were being carried out in the Regions. Elliot fortunately was very much more politically sensitive than his predecessor. As a long-standing member of the Carlton Club he knew that the Conservatives would insist upon changes in the railway set-up.

But Elliot's awareness of external forces was not always shared by the Members of the Executive, who sometimes seemed to be complacently solving yesterday's problems. Frank Pope, who had in fact been Hurcomb's nominee for the RE Chairmanship, but rejected by the Minister, initiated a greater insistence upon Commission participation in railway matters. His approach was based upon personal relationships rather than the written word; his views were strongly held but he was not very articulate on paper. Friendly (and preferably convivial) contacts were his chosen method of getting points across. I was appointed Secretary to a Committee of which Pope was Chairman. He sent for me and said: 'We are going to run this show as follows. At the first meeting, you will arrange a damned good lunch and we shall all get to know each other. At the second meeting, you will produce a draft of our final report. The rest of our meetings will be spent in getting your draft right'.

One of Pope's interests — which was shared by Sir Reginald Wilson, the forceful Comptroller of the Commission — was the cost of the train services still maintained on minor lines and branches. The Executive had set up two committees to review unremunerative lines and, where appropriate, make recommendations for closure. But in the absence of any determined policy on the part of the Executive as a whole, progress was slow. In fact, over the six years of the Executive's existence the route-mileage only fell from 19,639 to 19,222, or by 2.1 per cent.

In Northern Ireland, Pope had introduced diesel railcar services extensively and he was convinced that they were the answer to the problem of rural train services. He pressed the Executive to exploit their possibilities and the RE set up in August 1951 a rather oddly-named Light Weight Trains Committee, which reported with commendable speed in March 1952. It recommended that experimental schemes on a large scale should be introduced in Lincolnshire, the West Riding, and West Cumberland and on the Newcastle-Carlisle and Waverley routes. Substantial savings as well as increased train mileage were forecast.

Somewhat to the Commission's annoyance, the Executive seemed to drag its feet about implementing these schemes. This was not Elliot's fault, but arose from conservatism and pre-occupation with other matters on the part of Members and (it must be said) one or two Chief Regional Officers. Even after the Regional planning for the West Riding scheme had made some progress, in 1953 H.A. Short, the Chief Regional Officer, suddenly executed a volte-face and told the Executive he would prefer to drop the project. Elliot told him in no uncertain terms that this was out of the question.

Earlier that year a submission had been received by the Commission from the Executive (Riddles being its chief sponsor) for the construction of push-pull steam units for branch line services, rather than diesel railcars. This, not surprisingly, infuriated Pope.

By this time the first BR standard locomotives had appeared; in 1951 89 were built of five classes, 25 of them being Pacifics of the Class 7 Britannia type. One locomotive of this class was exhibited at the Festival of Britain, together with a main line diesel and one of the locomotives built for the Manchester-Sheffield-Wath electrification that was to open early in 1952. The Britannias were an immediate success on the Liverpool Street-Norwich service, where more powerful locomotives had long been needed. Standard departure times and a two-hour schedule between London and Norwich transformed this service and gave it temporarily a high place in the table of fastest booked runs on BR. The welcome by Eastern Region drivers for the Britannias was in marked contrast to the lack of enthusiasm shown by drivers on the Western Region, still unwilling to admit that Swindon design could be equalled, much less excelled, by anything produced by a committee at 222 Marylebone Road!

Also in 1951 the first standard passenger carriages appeared. They bore quite a strong resemblance to the last LMS carriages of the 1930s and also owed something to Bulleid's last corridor designs of the 1940s on the SR. They were conventional in interior lay-out, and, again echoing LMS policy, reduction in first cost had led to a bogie design that was to be a major handicap before a decade had passed. The BR standard bogie gave an acceptable ride at speeds up to about 60mph. At higher speeds, especially when a vehicle was approaching the end of a period between repairs, bogie hunting and violent lateral jerks were common especially on certain lengths of continuously welded track; this weakness was of course accentuated when diesel locomotives capable of running at 90mph for long stretches were introduced. The Mark I standard design was really out-of-date from its introduction; what was acceptable under pre-war conditions had become unacceptable within a few years of the building programme being launched.

It was to be 1964 before a major step forward was taken with a prototype Mark II train being put into service and by then the shortcomings of the Mark I stock had had serious commercial consequences for BR's Inter-City business.

Reference has been made to the slow progress made with standardising and installing the automatic warning system. If this had been in use on the London Midland main line from Euston in 1952, it would almost certainly have prevented the worst disaster on the railways since the terrible collision at Quintinshill in 1915, the double collision at Harrow & Wealdstone on 8 October. No fewer than 108 passengers, as well as train crews, lost their lives when an up sleeping car express from Perth overtook and collided with a local train from Tring to Euston as it was pulling out of the station, only seconds before a double-headed express from Euston to Liverpool and Manchester, running on the adjacent down line in the opposite direction, crashed into the wreckage caused by the first collision. The driver of the train from Perth had run through signals in a way that would almost certainly been prevented if aws had been installed. This terrible accident increased the pressure for a clear programme for installing aws and at last a full-scale experiment with the modified BR system was put in hand, equipping 54 locomotives.

Commercial policy and organisation were also, it was clear, soon going to be affected by the change of Government in October 1951. The Commission correctly foresaw that the Conservatives would have no use for integration. But it also knew that the new Government hankered for a return to something like the former railway companies in place of the Regions dominated by the Executive. This suited the Commission's book, since its Members were disenchanted with the Railway Executive and itched to take over direct control of the Regions. The BTC suggested to the new Minister of Transport that (in the words of the Annual Report for 1952) 'they could move towards a simpler form of organisation which, while not sacrificing the advantages and economies only to be secured by central control of certain essential matters, would lead to further decentralisation by devolution of authority to Regions, combined with the development of a road/rail service for freight traffic under a single commercial management'.

The Minister ignored this approach, but in May 1952 a White Paper was produced which forecast a Bill that would require the BTC to sell off its road haulage undertaking and decentralise its railway organisation. The first proposal was irrelevant to the transport needs of the nation, and the second was unnecessary as the Commission would wish to do this in any case. However, a Bill was introduced in July and became law as the Transport Act, 1953, in May next year. It provided for the abolition of the Railway Executive and required the BTC to prepare a scheme of organisation providing for statutory Area authorities to be set up, which would manage the railway Regions under the BTC. It also provided for a Road Haulage Disposals Board to be created with the task of de-nationalising British Road Services, thus putting the final nail in the coffin of road-rail integration.

So far as the railways were concerned, the prospect of new management was welcomed in the Regions. The Western Region saw this as a victory for GWR traditions which had had some effect upon the thinking of the Conservative Party. At a luncheon presided over by Frank Pope and attended by C.K. Bird, the Eastern Region CRO, a toast was drunk to closer contacts between the BTC and the Regions, and to the speedy disappearance of the 'intervening body', ie the Executive.

The Executive in fact was abolished (by a Ministerial Order) on 1 October 1953 and thereafter began a period of confusion and uncertainty that contrasted strangely with the rather rigid pattern enforced by the Executive. The wind of change had become a gale.

Above: Return to pre-war Pullman luxury: the Bournemouth Belle passes Wimbledon in 1947. (*C.R.L. Coles*). *Below:* A new named train on the GC line: the South Yorkshireman approaches Amersham in 1949. (*C.R.L. Coles*)

Above: Completion of the LNER's pre-war scheme for GE line electrification: the Ilford flyover with 'Shenfield' stock in 1949. (*British Rail*). *Below:* Before the high-class freight had begun to dwindle: a fast freight train leaves Camden Goods in 1950. (*British Rail*)

Chapter 8
Messing about with Diesels

There is plenty of room for controversy about the Railway Executive's traction policy up to 1953. On the one hand, it can be argued that the pre-occupation with designing standard steam locomotives was a disaster; it was irrelevant to the needs of the day, and was an exercise in nostalgia, which wasted valuable time and created many difficulties for the Executive's successors. On the other hand, it can be said the the RE inherited a number of diesel prototypes from the companies, none of which yet constituted a fully satisfactory type of main line locomotive; that these were tested over an extended period with results that were far from conclusive. Was this the fault of the designs, or was it due to any failure to carry out testing continuously and rigorously? Steam locomotive history is of course full of instances of new or unorthodox prototypes that were tested rather perfunctorily and then, when problems arose, were pushed away with a sigh of relief, to await scrapping after a decent interval spent shrouded under a tarpaulin!

The list of main line diesel (and gas turbine) locomotives inherited from the former companies, sometimes only as projects, and tested between 1948 and the end of the Railway Executive's existence, is as follows:

Type	HP	From	Ordered by	Delivered	Number
D/E Main Line CC	1,600	English Electric — Derby Works	LMS	1947/8	2
D/E Main Line 1CC1	1,750	English Electric — Ashford Works	SR	1950/1	2

cont'd overleaf

D/E Main Line 1CC1	2,000	English Electric — Brighton Works	SR	1954	1
D/E Mixed Traffic BB	827	Paxman BTH—NB Loco. Co	LMS	1950	1
D/Mechanical 'Fell' 4-8-4		Derby Works	LMS	1952	1
Gas turbine A1A—A1A		Brown Boveri	GWR	1950	1
Gas turbine CC		Metro-Vick	GWR	1952	1

It must be noted that this list excludes shunters. The LMS, and to a lesser extent the LNER, had experimented with diesel-electric shunters of the 0-6-0 type before the war and concluded that they showed substantial economies over steam shunting, largely due to their almost continuous availability. They had also proved reliable, largely no doubt owing to the fact that they were usually working far below their rated power output and to their low service mileages, often less than 30 miles a day (calculated on the basis of shunting hours).

The Railway Executive had accepted that they formed a useful back-up to steam traction, and by 1953 authority had been given by the Commission, on the recommendation of the Executive, for the building of 573 diesel-electric shunters over a period of five years, which would mean a complete change from steam to diesel traction in the most important marshalling yards. Meanwhile, between 1948 and 1953 (inclusive), a total of 139 diesel shunters (126 with electric, 11 with mechanical and two with hydraulic transmission) had been actually built for the Railway Executive, so that in this field there was continued if modest progress, although as nine types were involved, standardisation was still some way off. However, 187 of the 350hp diesel-electric type existed mostly in the LMS version.

At the end of 1953, the total number of diesel-electric locomotives — mostly shunters — on British Railways had risen to 242. The great question-mark therefore hung over the small assortment of main line diesels and the two gas turbine prototypes. It may be worth trying to trace their careers.

The two 1,600hp English Electric locomotives ordered by the LMS and delivered, one just before and one soon after nationalisation, probably had the longest and most successful working lives. No 10000 started its trials in January 1948 on the St Pancras-Manchester route. It had two six-wheel bogies described as a Co-Co wheel arrangement. Interestingly, it was reported that Crewe Works had just completed the first of two steam locomotives which were intended to compete with the diesel, a locomotive, named *Sir William A Stanier, FRS*, of the same general design as the existing 4-6-2 Stanier Coronation class. It included a number of features introduced by the CME of the LMS, H.G. Ivatt, intended to give increased availability, reduce maintenance costs and lengthen the period between heavy repairs. All axles were fitted with roller bearings and other refinements included a redesign of the reversing gear. The two locomotives, steam and diesel, were exhibited side by side at Euston, but no details of any subsequent competition seem to have been provided.

I enjoyed a front-end trip with No 10000 between St Pancras and Derby and it appeared to perform extremely well. It was reported that the weekly mileage achieved by the summer of that year had risen to 3,100. When the sister locomotive appeared, the two worked in multiple, producing 3,200hp, on the heaviest West Coast Anglo-Scottish expresses. In the autumn, Cecil J. Allen reported that 'for the first time in British locomotive history, a daily locomotive mileage of over 800 .... has been reached in Great Britain'. Allen reported that the performance of the twin diesels on the Royal Scot service was characterised by 'magnificent accelerative capacity'. He added that there had been an instance of a start from St Pancras, banked as usual by a steam carriage pilot, in which the tail end of the diesel-hauled train left the panting banker behind some distance before the latter had reached the end of the platform!

Later however the twins were put on less glamorous duties, namely hauling fitted freight trains between London and

Crewe. But in 1951 they were back in double harness on express passenger work. By this time experience of the type must have been pretty extensive.

Turning next to the locomotives ordered by the Southern Railway, the first of these, No 10201, was delivered at the end of 1950, and the second in August 1951, both having been built at Ashford Works. They were actually authorised before the two LMS locomotives, but various delays took place so that their delivery came a good deal later. Unlike the LMS twins, which were designed for mixed traffic working, the Southern locomotives were intended for passenger work only and had eight-wheel bogies of 1Co-Co1 wheel arrangement.

No 10202 was engaged, soon after delivery, in a twice-daily return working between Waterloo and Exeter Central, six days a week. In an enthusiastic comment Cecil J. Allen recorded in September 1952 what he described as 'terrific acceleration', 'the fastest time from Exeter to Sidmouth Junction that I have ever known' and running 'even at the highest speeds, of the most exemplary smoothness'. Subsequently exchanges were arranged, the LMS locomotives being transferred to the Southern Region, partly on account of difficulties with carriage heating during the winter. The third Southern main line diesel, also ordered before nationalisation, was uprated to 2000hp and built at Brighton Works in 1954. It was also 1Co-Co1 so far as wheel arrangement was concerned.

The generally satisfactory performance of these prototypes was not matched by two others both ordered by the LMS, namely the 827hp Bo-Bo mixed-traffic and the experimental Fell diesel-mechanical 4-8-4 named after the inventor of its complex mechanical drive Lt Col Fell. The former, No 10800, was delivered in July 1950 but proved unsatisfactory. The Paxman diesel engine was associated with British-Thompson-Houston electrical equipment, and the main contractor was the North British Locomotive Co Ltd. It was intended for branch line and local passenger services but never performed satisfactorily although fairly extensive trials took place on the Southern Region in 1952. The Executive engaged in a long and inconclusive correspondence with the three principal contractors regarding the shortcomings, which led nowhere.

The Fell locomotive, No 10100, was a brilliantly original attempt to apply mechanical transmission to diesel traction. It embodied four small diesel engines each of 400hp, driving through differential gears. By a method of supercharging, it attempted to avoid the problems of using a change-speed gearbox in connection with high-powered engines. It was delivered in mid-1951 and entered regular service on January 21, 1952. It performed quite well for a time on the steeply-graded Midland line between Derby and Manchester. Then in August 1952 it suffered severe damage to the gearbox and retired to the repair shops, from which it did not reappear.

Last (but not least in terms of cost) came the two gas-turbine locomotives ordered by the Great Western Railway, Nos 18000 and 18100. The first to be delivered was that built by Brown Boveri of Switzerland, in February 1950. It ran several hundred miles before some of the blading on the rotor of the air compressor developed defects and the first of several visits to repair shops took place; but it achieved some 41,000 miles in 1951, mainly on passenger and milk train service on the London-Bristol route.

The second, built by Metropolitan-Vickers Electrical Co Ltd, was delivered in December 1951. It was reputed to have done some good work, mainly on the Paddington-Plymouth and Paddington-Bristol routes. Cecil J. Allen described the running as excellent. But the BTC's Annual Report for 1952 stated that 'it is too early to come to definite conclusions about the development prospects of this type of traction on British Railways'. They remained in the railway stock lists until 1957/58, the Metro-Vick machine having been converted into a prototype electric locomotive for the 25kV electrification of the Manchester-Crewe main line, and the Swiss-built one having been handed over to the Research Department for electrical experimental work, minus the gas turbine. Later it returned to Switzerland where it is still in existence as a test unit.

E.S. Cox, in *Locomotive Panorama*, has summed up the reasons for the failure of gas turbine propulsion on British Railways as follows: 'The over-riding and fundamental fault of any gas turbine as prime mover is its poor part-load efficiency and therefore fuel consumption. Traffic conditions on BR are such that low load factors prevail and the diesel, whose specific fuel consumption hardly varies over the whole power range, is ideally suited to such conditions. The gas turbine, having twice the specific fuel rate at 10% load as at full load, is at a hopeless disadvantage.' (Cox was writing before the decision was taken to abandon gas turbine propulsion for the Advanced Passenger Train, but his words seem to have been borne out by experience in most countries, except in France, where the SNCF appears to have accepted uneconomic rates of fuel consumption in its high-speed turbo-trains coded ETG and RTG.)

In conclusion, what can one say about the 1948-53 period of dabbling with diesel traction? The Railway Executive did not order a single main line diesel during its six years of existence. It seems to have accepted the legacy of prototypes from the companies with a marked lack of enthusiasm at the top level though in the Regions testing often evoked keen interest. Performance of the two LMS English Electric locomotives and of the Southern trio seems to have been good enough to have justified a large-scale development, possibly on the lines of the LNER East Coast Main Line project which the Executive, bent on designing standard steam locomotives, seems to have consigned to the scrap heap without examination.

The letter which I had drafted from Hurcomb to Missenden dated 13 April 1948 (already mentioned on page 46) contained the following sentences:

> It seems to me that the question of the future form of traction —
> whether it is to be steam, electricity, Diesel-electric, Diesel-
> mechanical, or gas turbine — is probably the most important
> long-term problem facing the railways to-day, and it is of course
> closely linked with the future price ratios and availability of the
> different fuels . . . .

A large main line electrification scheme [ex-LNER Manchester-Sheffield-Wath] is in progress. The Executive also have in hand proposals for prolonged technical trials of both Diesel-mechanical and gas turbine main line locomotives. But as regards Diesel-electric traction, there seems to be a disparity. We are still experimenting as though there were no large fund of technical knowledge and experience upon which to draw, and as though our engineers had not been studying the characteristics (as I assume they have been doing) of this form of traction for the past twenty years.

Whilst American practice admittedly requires to be interpreted in the light of the smaller loads, shorter average length of haul, and more restricted loading gauge in this country, there should be no major technical questions which are quite unfamiliar.

Where our experience is lacking, is in the true level of maintenance and operating costs under British conditions, and the effects upon operating methods of turning over a complete group of services to diesel-electric traction. And only a large-scale experiment can give us the answer to these questions.

For this reason I was disappointed to read in Slim's letter of 23rd March that so limited an experiment as that now in hand in the London Midland Region is all that the Executive apparently contemplate at the moment.

You will remember that in the summer of 1947 the L.N.E.R. announced that they had prepared a scheme for the dieselisation of the Anglo-Scottish East Coast services, involving the construction of 25 single units in replacement of 32 "Pacific" type express passenger engines. Maintenance facilities were to be provided at London and Edinburgh, entirely separate from the steam locomotive facilities.

The Commission would, I think, like to know whether it is the fact that this scheme has now been shelved and whether the Executive have come to conclusions which differ radically from those which were formed by the L.N.E.R. Board last year. I cannot help feeling, however, that until a major scheme of the kind has been put into operation, we shall not have sufficient actual experience of the capabilities and costs of Diesel-electric traction in relation to steam and other forms of traction.

When eventually the Executive replied, in the following December, it was merely to inform the Commission that a Committee on Types of Motive Power had been set up.

That Committee eventually reported in October 1951 and it went far to meet, if belatedly, Hurcomb's point, since it recommended that there should be a trial main line diesel conversion scheme notionally involving the provision of 100 locomotives in the 2,000hp class. But the Commission waited in vain for the Executive to take any steps to implement this constructive proposal.

Had that taken place, and had diesel traction been progressively developed, the later reaction against the Executive's policy, or lack of policy, would not have been so violent in 1954 and the immediately succeeding years. There would have been a foundation upon which to plan a progressive and probably slower changeover from steam. So, ironically, the RE steam lobby probably was a main cause of the too precipitate movement away from steam under the 1955 Modernisation Plan.

Chapter 9

Sparks Effect

The Railway Executive has been heavily criticised, with much justification, for its steam locomotive building policy and its relative indifference to the possibilities of diesel main line locomotives. Having said this, it should be added that the fault lay more in the organisation than with individuals, and also that electric traction was not subject to the same indifference as diesel traction.

R.A. Riddles has borne the brunt of the criticism; in fact, the functional system was probably to blame. It placed a dedicated and enthusiastic steam locomotive engineer in charge of the whole traction field; his official responsibilities covered 'mechanical engineering, electrical engineering, road motor engineering and scientific research'. It should have been the collective responsibility of the Executive to determine traction policy; if this had been done and a balanced programme of development laid down, no doubt Riddles would have successfully planned a better, and in the event a longer, role for steam than was actually to exist owing to the violent reaction in 1954 against what was considered the over-conservatism of the Executive.

It must also be said that Riddles seems to have accepted that ultimately electric traction must come to predominate, though not in his working lifetime. The controversial point was simply this: belief that steam must continue to fill the gap for the foreseeable future, whereas the BTC Modernisation Plan insisted that steam was no longer able to meet the demands of a modern railway, and that, pending electrification, diesels must fill the gap.

Within the limits set by Government controls on investment, the Railway Executive had developed a considerable interest in suburban electrification, in addition to its inheritance of the LNER's Manchester-Sheffield-Wath and Liverpool Street-Shenfield projects. In May 1948 the BTC had arranged for a joint British Railways and London Transport Committee, chaired by C.M. Cock, Chief Electrical Engineer of the Executive, to be set up to consider the system (or systems) of electrification to be adopted in future projects, reviewing in particular the conclusions of the Pringle Committee of 1927 which had proposed direct current at either 1,500 volts with overhead collection for general use, and 750 volts third rail for certain areas. The Cock Committee broadly confirmed this, but did not rule out the possibility of using, as it put it, 'single-phase alternating current at 50 cycles or a lower frequency for secondary lines with light traffic, subject to the proviso that it is not prejudicial to operation on adjacent lines equipped with a standard system'.

This opened the way for the decision taken in 1951 to use the short Lancaster-Morecambe-Heysham line, which the Midland Railway had electrified many years ago on the 6,600 volts 25-cycle single-phase system, as a testing-ground for electrification at the industrial frequency of 50 cycles (Hz), which seemed to offer important advantages, especially in cutting down the cost of the distribution network. This system had already been tried in Hungary as early as 1934 and the SNCF was proceeding to install it on an important main line in Eastern France.

The old electric equipment on the Heysham and Morecambe line was life-expired and the electric trains had been replaced by steam services, when it was arranged to try 50 Hz ac, using superannuated prototype vehicles from the former Euston and Broad Street suburban electrification which had seen little use since withdrawal of Willesden-Earl's Court services during the second world war.

So far as concrete proposals were concerned, in January 1949 the Executive set up a headquarters committee to prepare a scheme for electrification of the London Tilbury & Southend line, thereby suggesting the redemption of a promise exacted by Parliament from the former Midland Railway when it gobbled up the LT&S Railway under the nose of the Great Eastern in 1912. This headquarters committee was not exactly a favourite with the Eastern Region's management, which would have preferred to work out its own proposals; however, it reported in August 1950, with an outline scheme based on 1,500 volts dc with overhead contact. Progress was slow and the planning was overtaken in June 1953 by the Eastern Region's own proposal to extend the existing Shenfield electrification to Chelmsford and Southend (Victoria), which the Region plausibly argued should precede and eventually complement the LT&S project. This was agreed by the Executive and the Commission. The Eastern Region officers, largely inspired by the drive and energy of A. J. White, Assistant CRO and later Assistant GM, pressed on with other proposals, including the lines from Liverpool Street to Enfield and Chingford, Hertford and Bishops Stortford (usually known as the 'Chenford' scheme), as well as the development of a project by a joint RE and Regional committee for electrification of the Great Northern suburban lines from King's Cross. (This project came to a standstill, partly because of a suggestion that a Great Northern main line scheme ought to be developed, partly because of the formidable problem of remodelling King's Cross and its approaches, so that in the event it was not to be realised until the late 1970s.) The Eastern Region was however also looking at the possibilities of electrifying between Bishops Stortford, Cambridge and March (Whitemoor); and Chelmsford to Ipswich, including the Clacton, Harwich and Felixstowe branches. The Region's planning resources were in fact over-extended by attempts to develop all these projects more or less simultaneously.

The Southern Region had inherited a comprehensive scheme from the Southern Railway for the elimination of steam traction from the area east of a line drawn from Reading to Portsmouth. It was envisaged that the principal lines would be equipped with the standard Southern third rail system, while the secondary lines would be turned over to diesel traction. By the time the Executive was abolished in 1953 virtually nothing had been done to implement this proposal.

In Scotland, the Commission had appointed in 1949 a committee 'to consider and report on the transport requirements of Glasgow and the adjacent areas'. The Chairman was Sir Robert Inglis who was relinquishing his position as Chief of the Transport Division of the Control Commission for Germany, and who had been a former Divisional General Manager of the Scottish Area of the LNER. The other members included the General Manager of Scottish Omnibuses Ltd as well as three railway officers. The Inglis Report, as it was known, appeared in October 1951 and, while it reviewed the road situation, devoted most attention to railway proposals including the electrification from Queen Street (Low Level) to Helensburgh and Airdrie and branches, and Glasgow Central to Cathcart Circle with branches to Neilston High and Kirkhill.

This was therefore broadly the situation when the Commission took over from the Executive. The RE had brought to completion the two projects inherited from the LNER and of its own volition had developed a number of schemes for (mainly) suburban electrification, but little material progress had been made with these. The two Eastern Region Southend routes were in the lead, and encouraging noises were being made by the engineers about the prospects for 25kV ac 50 Hz traction, based on the results at Morecambe/Heysham. The picture was however confused, with ideas being floated for extending Manchester/Sheffield-Wath westwards over the Cheshire Lines and eastwards to Lincoln and Annesley — ultimately, it was even suggested to Aylesbury and London (Marylebone)! Other ideas included the former GN and GE Joint Line from March to Lincoln and Doncaster, while the London Midland threw in a first bid for consideration of Euston to Birmingham, Liverpool and Manchester.

It was not until the launching of the Modernisation Plan at the end of 1954 that the vaguer of these suggestions were to be eliminated and some priorities of a more realistic nature worked out.

All this rather unco-ordinated (and partly fruitless) effort seems curious in an Executive headed by two successive Chairmen from the Southern, the first railway to be 'sold' on electrification. Moreover in October 1951 the Executive had at last produced a substantial Report on Types of Motive Power, by a committee set up in December 1948 in belated response to Hurcomb's letter of April in that year to Missenden. The principal recommendation of this committee, chaired by J.L. Harrington, was that, so far as main line electrification was concerned, there should be detailed planning and costing of a scheme for the electrification of the Great Northern main line to (at least) Grantham and Nottingham 'to be carried out as early as possible consistent with the capital investment and the labour and materials situations'. This recommendation was not implemented because of a number of factors, which between them help to explain the lack of any clear policy on electrification at this time. First, there was uncertainty as to whether planning was to be a headquarters or a Regional function. Then, there was undoubtedly a shortage both of planning resources and of overall investment allocations. Lastly, there was no clear lead given from the top, where the relevant Executive Member's personal support and impetus were essential. This was only really evident in the case of the London Tilbury & Southend project, developed under Cock's chairmanship.

So far as the Regions were concerned, the Western and the North Eastern were not interested, and the London Midland only made token gestures in favour of electrification. The Scottish Region was closely involved in the Inglis Committee proposals for Glasgow but lacked technical experience and resources. The Southern, which one would have expected to spearhead the drive to extend electrification, was occupied in modernising the distribution network of its existing system so as to take high-tension current from the grid at the industrial frequency of 50 Hz instead of 25 Hz from its own power station at Durnsford Road, Wimbledon. It was also lengthening the trains on the most intensively used suburban services from eight to ten cars, involving track and signalling re-modelling as well as platform lengthening.

That left only the Eastern, firmly convinced of the virtues of electrification but short of resources, planning and technical, to develop all the projects with which its management was toying.

None of this really satisfied the Commission, and particularly Hurcomb, whose support for electrification in principle sprang largely from the fact that before the war he had for some years held an important post as Chairman of the Central Electricity Board. Incidentally, he felt that it was wrong, as a general policy, for the railways to generate their own supplies; they ought to buy electricity in bulk from the grid.

There were however growing signs that railwaymen were looking at electrification in a broader way than had generally been the case before the war. Then, apart from suburban net-works, the argument had generally been that main line electrification *per se* would not generate any traffic. It was therefore only normally justifiable to improve operation where special conditions — above all, heavy gradients — existed. This had been the case made out for Manchester-Sheffield-Wath with its heavy trans-Pennine coal traffic. It had induced the Great Western to examine the case for Taunton-Penzance, though the savings here had offered no convincing argument.

Now electrification was beginning to be seen as the most important single element in a modernised railway system, and one that might not merely help to retain existing traffic but attract new business by offering a faster, more reliable and cleaner service — in fact, the 'sparks effect' which often defied quantification when schemes were being prepared but which never failed to appear once electrification had been carried out. The Southern's experiences had of course always proved this, but some railwaymen on other systems had been inclined to argue that the Southern's circumstances were special if not unique. Now however the results of post-war electrifications showed that the sparks effect could be relied upon to appear almost anywhere. Completion of the Liverpool Street-Shenfield scheme, for instance, had shown an increase of 48.5 per cent in passenger journeys and 40.8 per cent in receipts for the nine months immediately after electrification, compared with the same nine months in the previous year, before electrification.

And although electrification made slow headway, steam's Indian summer was not being marked by specially fine weather. Despite some excellent and well-publicised performances by some of Riddles's BR standard types — the 4-6-2 Britannias and the Class 9 2-10-0s on exceptional occasions used on express passenger work with their astonishing turn of speed were examples — the underlying difficulties created by unsatisfactory coal supplies, staff shortages and inadequate maintenance facilities at many depots, persisted and handicapped management in the attempt to present the quality of service that an increasingly competitive market demanded. A new look at the whole traction situation was overdue.

Chapter 10

Under New Management

Towards the end of 1953, there were great upheavals in the nationalised transport scene. With the disappearance of the Railway Executive, the British Transport Commission was suddenly enlarged to enable it to take over the management of British Railways as well as of the other Executives, except London Transport, the only one to survive. The BTC moved into 222 Marylebone Road, and a vast 'general post' took place inside the building as new men arrived and struggled to discover just what their powers and responsibilities were going to be while the survivors of the Railway Executive looked on with some horror.

In the Regions there may have been rejoicing; at the top, there was quite unparalleled confusion. For instance, nobody, for several months, found anything at all to do for an unfortunate senior officer, the former Secretary of the Railway Executive. He retained his title, although the Executive had disappeared; that was all. Day by day he arrived at his office, read *The Times* for as long as possible, and then quit his empty desk.

The Commission changed after the retirement of Lord Hurcomb (he had received the title in 1950). Sir William Wood also retired, but the other members of the Commission were re-appointed; to them was added J.C.L. Train, the only Member of the RE to go 'upstairs'. As previously mentioned, he had cannily managed to keep clear of the Executive's more controversial policies. A notable addition to the full-time Members was Sir Reginald Wilson, the former Comptroller, whose energy and fertile brain were soon to be much more closely involved with railway management.

The Railway Executive members fared variously in the re-

Right: The East Coast floods: testing a temporary bridge in 1948. (*Crown copyright National Railway Museum*). *Below:* BR's worst disaster since Quintinshill: the Harrow & Wealdstone accident of 8 October 1952. (*BBC/Hulton Picture Library*)

Above: The pioneer twin main line diesels ordered by the LMS, Nos 10000 and 10001, passing Whitmore troughs in 1949 with the up Royal Scot. (*Real Photographs*). *Below:* A fascinating failure: the ingenious 'Fell' diesel-mechanical express locomotive in 1951. (*Crown copyright National Railway Museum*)

shuffle. Sir Michael Barrington-Ward (B-W had been knighted in 1952) and R.A. Riddles retired. Three Members stepped down into the position of Chief Officers under the Commission. W.P. Allen became Chief of Establishment and Staff; David Blee, Chief of Commercial Services; and Sir Daril Watson, Chief of General Services, later Secretary-General.

But by far the most important new appointment was that of the new BTC Chairman, General Sir Brian Robertson. His arrival in September 1953 soon caused legends to fly around the building. Tall, austere, shy and formidable, his prolonged silences could be disconcerting. He came with a great reputation as a military administrator in occupied Germany; he was the son of the first Field-Marshal of the British Army to have started as a ranker, Sir William Robertson. His father's toughness and utter dedication were fully reproduced in Brian Robertson. He accepted the BTC Chairmanship as a duty and applied to it the military doctrine that the Commander-in-Chief must, from the moment he is appointed, be seen to command. This left little time for learning about the old complex railway industry of which he had suddenly become the head.

John Elliot might reasonably have expected to move from the defunct Railway Executive to the Commission. But the BTC was not a railway, it was a transport conglomerate, and politicians and civil servants agreed that it must be led by a supposedly impartial 'outsider', not by a railwayman. So they awarded Elliot the 'consolation prize' of the Chairmanship of London Transport, coupled with a knighthood. (Elliot subsequently had very happy relations, untinged by any suspicion of envy, with Robertson.)

In the general turmoil at headquarters after Robertson arrived, an interim organisation was hastily set up for the railways. Frank Pope was put in charge of operating and commercial matters, J.C.L. Train of technical and engineering affairs.

These Duomvirs of the railways had a certain amount of fun at headquarters, while the Chief Regional Officers became

Chief Regional Managers and Regional pride was thereby given a taste of things to come.

But all these upheavals were not really very relevant to the growing problems that the railways faced. Early in 1953, as a result of conversations between Pope, Wilson and Elliot, a group of RE officers under the Chairmanship of J.L. Harrington, Chief Officer (Marine and Administration) had been charged with outlining a plan for spending £500 millions on railway development. This was a sort of rehearsal for the Modernisation Plan of 1954-55. In April 1953 the quick outline was complete, covering electrification (£160 million) as the major item, and all-round improvements in most other directions including (surprisingly) £40m. for 'helicopter terminals and services'. The report proposed that terminal stations in nine cities should be adapted as combined rail/helicopter terminals, with a view to the establishment of helicopter services not merely within Great Britain but also with Ireland and near Continental countries. This proposal was obviously in some way a bid to recover the interest in air transport which the railways had lost after the war under nationalisation, when they were obliged to divest themselves of their airline investments. However, the confusion following reorganisation prevented anything being done about this outline plan, at any rate for the time being.

Meanwhile, life in the Regions had to continue, whatever the power struggles at the top. The Chief Regional Managers experienced a brief 'honeymoon', dealing for the most part with Pope and Train on matters requiring sanction from higher authority. The new Chairman was an Olympian figure who, though he visited the Regions, was preoccupied for the time being with problems of organisation. His brooding over this subject eventually produced a set-up so complicated and hierarchical that nobody really understood how to make it work. The Transport Act 1953 had required the BTC to prepare a scheme for setting up Area 'authorities', which were clearly intended (by Section 16 of the Act) to be as much like the old railway companies as was feasible under nationalisation.

Robertson produced a scheme which the Government published in a White Paper in July 1954, and it was embodied in a Ministerial Order which Parliament approved on 24 November in the same year. Under it, the Regions acquired 'Area Boards', from 1 January 1955, and the Chief Regional Managers became General Managers. The interim period was over.

Anyone who had dreamt that the Great Western Railway, for instance, was about to be reborn was soon to be disillusioned. Headquarters officers multiplied and the General Managers who might have thought life would be easier, with just an Area Board Chairman to deal with, soon discovered that a hierarchy of specialists at 222 was determined to have some say in running the Regions. These gentlemen were grouped in two levels, the lower being the British Railways Central Staff of departmental experts, the upper level being the so-called 'General Staff' whom Sir Brian Robertson had set up partly on the Army model. Over and above this, there were other bodies — committees, sub-commissions and advisory bodies — all involving themselves in railway affairs.

In consequence, a Regional General Manager who wanted authority for a proposal emanating from one of his own departmental officers, might see it examined by:

Area Board
Relevant officers of BR Central Staff
General Staff of the Commission
Railway Sub-Commission
Committee of the Commission
The Commission itself.

Life had become very complicated!

A symbol of the new form of headquarters management was the new board room which Robertson ordered for the meetings of the Commission. The Executive Members had sat round tables grouped to form a rectangle in a moderate-sized meeting-room. The new board room was laid out like the council chamber of a major local authority, with the Chairman in the centre of a row of desks facing several tiers of seats opposite in a half-moon. Over the Chairman's head a large plaque displayed the BTC armorial bearings.

The psychological effect was considerable. Proceedings became much more formal and the large number of officials attending, as well as Area Board Chairmen and General Managers, meant that debate had to be closely controlled. Robertson's formidable presence in the chair rather discouraged the cut-and-thrust of discussion and people normally spoke only when invited to do so, and then were encouraged to be brief. The Chairman's summing-up was always impressive but sometimes one felt that the root of the matter had not been penetrated.

Even so, the railways continued to run and some real progress was recorded. The Anglo-Scottish train services were speeded up by the restoration of a maximum line speed of 90mph over much of the West Coast route in 1953, and on the East Coast the non-stop Elizabethan came down to 6¾ hours between King's Cross and Waverley — still 45 minutes slower than the pre-war Coronation with two stops.

In fact, after eight years of peace, something approaching pre-war standards of train running was beginning to appear. The Royal Scot between Euston and Glasgow had 30 minutes clipped off its time; the 7.50 am from King's Cross to Leeds and Bradford was timed at 65.9mph over the 124.1 miles from Hitchin to Doncaster, start to stop, the fastest run in Great Britain. The pre-war standard two-hour timings between London and Bristol, and London and Birmingham re-appeared.

Overnight passengers benefitted from the introduction of the new third class sleeping cars, providing two berths to a compartment with full bedding and washing facilities, compared with the former rather spartan lying-down accomodation and four berths to a compartment.

Commercial activities included the operation of the Starlight Specials between London and Scotland at specially low fares (£3.50 return) designed to attract students and other price-conscious travellers. There was no sleeping accommodation on these trains but an all-night service of refreshments, a forerunner of the discotheques on some USA all-night trains in later years.

In 1953 the Commission also recorded with some complacency the fact that more train miles had been run than in the previous year but operating efficiency, as measured by train miles per train engine hour, and wagon miles per total engine hour, had improved. The number of locomotives, carriages and wagons under or awaiting repair also declined.

In the same year the new Woodhead tunnel was completed and a decision was taken to extend the Liverpool Street-Shenfield electrification to Chelmsford and Southend (Victoria), associated with the London Tilbury & Southend electrification, for which planning had been in hand for some time. There were substantial improvements at Euston including the restoration of the Great Hall to something like its original state before it had been disfigured during LMS days by the one-storey wooden enquiry offices in the middle of the floor.

But despite these signs of modest progress, there was restlessness among the new railway chieftains and a desire to strike out in new directions. Of course, the Commission had to cope with an enormous backlog of tasks created by the Transport Act, 1953, including road haulage de-nationalisation and the absorption into itself of the Executives, and could not concentrate solely upon railway problems. But there was also cause for concern at the rise in costs and a fall in net traffic receipts. These had been hitherto rising since 1949; now for the first time there was a drop, from £39.6 million to £35.1m. It foreshadowed, though no-one believed it at the time, the long slide into deficit.

Among the members of the Commission there were several who were anxious to see rapid new developments in British Railways, above all, H.P. Barker, a part-time Member with an industrial background. His restless inquiring mind and deep involvement in modern technology had chafed at the conservatism, as it seemed, of the Railway Executive. He contributed various papers on the impact of new technology which always evoked interest if not agreement. So by the mid-1950s the railways were being pulled in different ways. The new Area Boards were finding their feet and enjoying the sensation of running the Regions. The Olympian Sir Brian was in fact a great compromiser, holding the balance between Regional and Headquarters powers with considerable skill.

A small sign of the times was Sir Brian's decision that company liveries could be restored to a limited extent, nominally on named express trains. Great Western chocolate and cream reappeared on the Western Region, and LMS red on the London Midland. The latter was also used on the Eastern, North Eastern and Scottish Regions. The Southern retained green, although of different shade, for multiple-unit trains and reverted to green for locomotive-hauled stock most of which had ultimately succumbed to red and cream or all maroon.

Sir Brian Robertson had early on expressed his dislike of the 'bicycling lion' emblem and he approached the College of Arms for a grant of arms to the Commission. This, when it was eventually completed, was illustrated in the BTC Annual Report for 1956: it was a most complex affair, embodying a shield displaying wheels, wavy lines for water, and a portcullis and chains for the docks; a helmet and assorted trimmings. Also there were no fewer than *three* lions in a triangle, the topmost one holding up a wheel in its paws. It also included the Great Central Railway motto which the LNER had adopted, *Forward*. However, moving forward by itself was obviously considered insufficient and *Velociter* and *Securiter* also appeared on scrolls!

This jolly effort was scarcely practicable for use on the sides of locomotives or carriages, because of the mass of detail which it included. However, one element, the lion in a sit-up-and-beg position holding a wheel out for general admiration, was extracted and used by itself, sometimes encircled by a sort of garter to form a badge that had a vague resemblance at a distance to the old Midland wyvern and, when applied against a background of LMS red, was by no means unpleasing — a vast improvement on the under-nourished descendant of the Wembley lion and, many thought nostalgically in later years, really more decorative than the back-and-forth double arrow symbol which eventually displaced it in the 1960s.

If liveries and totems indicated some atmosphere of uncertainty, that was certainly characteristic of the early 1950s. The first real signs of the long-awaited Great Leap Forward (as Chairman Mao would have expressed it) came with the Modernisation Plan launched at the beginning of 1955.

Chapter 11

Modernisation at Last

When some sort of order had begun to emerge from the confusion which followed the abolition of the Railway Executive, and the Commission had time to take a hard look at the railways, the position was found to be unsatisfactory. Freight traffic was falling while costs were rising (wages costs rose by £18 million a year in 1954) and the effect on the Commission's overall financial position was likely to be serious. Ministers had expected the Conservative Government's transport legislation to show improved, not worsened results, even though its Act involved denationalisation of the profitable road haulage side. Sir Brian Robertson was soon asked what steps he proposed to take to rectify the unfavourable trend.

His answer was to launch the railway Modernisation Plan, published in January 1955. The theme of the Plan was set out in the Introduction, which admitted that 'British Railways to-day are not working at full efficiency, mainly owing to their past inability to attract enough capital investment to keep their physical equipment up to date. The Plan aims to produce a thoroughly modern system, able fully to meet both current traffic requirements and those of the foreseeable future. It is based on the premise that its main components shall be capable of being started within five years and completed within fifteen years.'

The time-scale foreshadowed in the last sentence proved remarkably accurate; the years 1960/70 were in fact to be the great decade of change within BR, though not always in the direction that the Plan anticipated.

The Plan was devised by a committee of headquarters and Regional officers, with sub-committees covering the main functional components. I was assigned to the Methods of

Traction Sub-Committee, whose deliberations were the most difficult and sometimes controversial. The arguments raged mainly over the future of steam. There was little disagreement that, in the long term, electrification was the right solution, and that as much electrification as was possible with the limited resources in sight should be written into the Plan. But where feelings ran high was on the question whether steam should continue to fill the gap, pending electrification, or whether diesel traction must take over in the meantime. Roland Bond, a fine engineer and a delightful person, ably commanded the rearguard action, arguing forcefully that steam was cheap, and well understood; it could sometimes show availability figures at least as good as those of any diesels hitherto in use; high performance steam locomotives could challenge the diesel, and all that was needed was more money for better maintenance facilities.

Against this, the 'modernists' argued that all the long-term factors were adverse to steam including the supply of suitable coal, labour willing to undertake the heavy and disagreeable work at steam motive power depots, and the need for better traction performance not as a matter for special demonstration runs but day in and day out. In the end they carried the day and the published Plan contained the words 'the Commission accordingly propose to build no new express passenger or suburban steam locomotives after the 1956 programme and to terminate the building of all new steam locomotives within a few years .... The Commission are agreed that, in broad terms, it is not a question of choosing between electricity and diesel traction, but rather of combining the two to the best advantage .... But the key factor .... is the volume of civil and signal engineering works that are involved; and there is therefore a limit to the amount of electrification that it appears practicable to complete within the period covered by the Plan. This amount of work has been provided for. As regards the remainder of the principal main-line services, it is intended to introduce diesel traction as quickly as possible.'

The actual electrification projects mentioned in the Plan

comprised (i) the Eastern Region suburban schemes, namely the LT&S and the Liverpool Street routes already in hand, together with the Great Northern suburban lines; (ii) the Glasgow suburban lines; (iii) the Kent Coast lines of the Southern Region; (iv) *Both* the Eastern Region main line to Doncaster, Leeds and (possibly) York, *and* the London Midland lines from Euston to Birmingham, Manchester and Liverpool; (v) extension of the Eastern Region Liverpool Street electrification from Chelmsford to Ipswich and branches.

The remainder of the Plan was less controversial. There was general agreement that the time and the opportunity had come to get rid of the small loose-coupled hand-braked goods wagon; to replace steam trains on branch line services by diesel multiple-units; to improve the permanent way and structures, and to extend both colour-light signalling and automatic train control.

Later critics have attacked the decision that a great deal of money must be spent on the construction or reconstruction of some 55 marshalling yards (aimed at closing or partially closing some 150 existing yards) and spending £50 millions on new or reconstructed goods stations for wagon-load traffic. There was already a significant drop in general wagon-load traffic compared with 1948, though perhaps not enough to justify extreme pessimism. But it was hoped to reverse this trend by providing better service through the reduction in trip working between many small yards, which caused delays and increased the possibilities of errors in marshalling.

The summary budget of the Plan was described as follows:

First, the track and signalling must be improved to make higher speeds possible over trunk routes, and to provide for better utilisation of the physical assets; there will be an extended use of colour-light signalling, track circuits and automatic train control, the further introduction of power-operated signal boxes, and the installation of centralised traffic control where conditions are suitable, and the extended use of modern telecommunication services .... £210 million.

Second, steam must be replaced as a form of motive power, electric or diesel traction being rapidly introduced as may be most

suitable in the light of the development of the Plan over the years; this will involve the electrification of large mileages of route, and the introduction of several thousand electric or diesel locomotives
....£345 million.

Third, much of the existing steam-drawn passenger rolling stock must be replaced, largely by multiple-unit electric or diesel trains; the remaining passenger rolling stock, which will be drawn by locomotives (whether electric, diesel or steam), must be modernised; the principal passenger stations and parcels depots will also require considerable expenditure ...... £285 million.

Fourth, the freight services must be drastically remodelled. Continuous brakes will be fitted to all freight wagons, which will lead to faster and smoother operation of freight traffic; marshalling yards and goods terminal facilities will be re-sited and modernised, and in particular the number of marshalling yards will be greatly reduced. Larger wagons will be introduced, particularly for mineral traffic, and loading and unloading appliances will require extensive modernisation in consequence .... £365 million.

Fifth, expenditure will be required on sundry other items, including improvements at the packet ports, staff welfare, office mechanisms, etc; and a sum of at least £10 million for development and research work will be associated with the Plan, making a total of .... £ 35 million

TOTAL .... £1,240 million

SAY   £1,200 million

The draft Plan having been built up from a series of sub-committee reports, did not read like a consistent document. I was given the task of editing and where necessary writing in new material to produce a readable submission, and even to-day am complacent enough to feel that a good deal of the argument still reads reasonably well. The Plan is often criticised for being backward-looking, for trying to reinstate the pre-war railway rather than build the new system for the years up to the end of the century. In fact, the Plan forecast that 'there will also be a substantial expansion in container transport, and other technical developments for the transfer of traffic between road and rail'; and on the passenger side admitted that 'certain other traffics, which are now carried at disproportionately high costs and are inherently more suited for road transport, will be gradually transferred to road'.

The real trouble with the Plan was its timing. In one sense it came too late; had it been launched immediately after the end of the war, when so many Continental countries were energetically starting to reconstruct on modern lines their war-damaged railways, the quality of service might have improved sufficiently to stave off much of the flight of traffic away from the railways. The heavy investments in goods terminals, wagons and marshalling yards would have had more justification than in 1955 when the writing was already on the wall, with the expansion of road freight transport.

If on the other hand the Plan had been delayed until after the Beeching 'Re-shaping', it can plausibly be argued that various components would have taken different shapes and a good deal of money would have been saved or more profitably directed. Some white elephants such as Kingmoor Yard or the Bletchley flyover would never have been acquired.

It was, for once, an agreeable surprise that the Government of the day welcomed the Plan very quickly; speaking in the House of Commons the month (February 1955) after the Plan was published, the Chancellor of the Exchequer (then Mr. R.A. Butler) said 'it is in the interests of the country that more money should be put into transport .... our policy is to proceed with the modernisation of the railways'. The Plan really involved just an increase, for a number of years, in the investment permitted to BR, on the one hand; and on the other, the addition to schemes already in the pipeline of a number of desirable projects which otherwise would have remained pigeon-holed. Self-contained profit and loss accounts and balance sheets for the Plan were never feasible.

In the event, drawing up the Plan was comparatively easy; the real difficulties arose when a start had to be made upon implementing it.

Chapter 12

Re-appraisals:
Agonizing and Otherwise

The later 1950s constituted a period in which the railways began to move into the contemporary scene instead of trying to re-create pre-war conditions. Unfortunately this process was accompanied by a slide into financial deficit which had never been foreseen. It was a period of struggle in every way — struggle to implement the Modernisation Plan, struggle between the Regions and the central organisation, struggle to discover whether railways could continue to be financially viable or must become State pensioners.

Perhaps the first visible sign of the new outlook was the introduction of diesel multiple-units on lightly-loaded branch line services, which really got under way in 1954 with schemes for the West Riding of Yorkshire and Cumberland and with many others in the pipeline. A sign of the times was the variation in design of units to meet Regional specifications, which sometimes seemed capricious. But it was Sir Brian's policy to pay regard to Area Board requests, whatever the BR Central Staff might say!

The other components of the Plan had to be worked out in some detail by specialist groups, and it was immediately apparent that technical resources were going to be inadequate; more staff would have to be recruited and trained. The slender economic studies underlying the Plan had to be strengthened by a national freight traffic survey forecasting the demand over every section of route, upon which was to be based a national marshalling yards plan and a modernised wagon fleet. Sadly, these forecasts when made proved over-optimistic. Freight traffic in the 'merchandise and livestock' category, where road competition was felt most keenly, fell in 1956 to no more than 85 per cent of the 1948 figure. Only the bulk traffics, mainly for the coal, iron and steel industries, were holding up well.

On the passenger side, while the replacement of pre-war stock was speeded up, and the building of non-corridor locomotive-hauled compartment stock at last came to an overdue end, the basic corridor coach designs continued to be the Mark I type, produced soon after nationalisation; the first Mark II stock did not appear in any quantity until after 1964.

Most attention was of course devoted to the great changeover in motive power, which also threw up large programmes of physical works on the ground, especially where electrification was involved. Platforms had to be lengthened and stations reconstructed; signalling changed from semaphore to colour-light; new carriage-cleaning and servicing depots installed; and track strengthening was widely needed to cope with more intensive services.

Even the diesel schemes involved considerable provision of new servicing facilities coupled with the progressive elimination of steam motive power depots and turntables, coaling stages, water cranes, track water troughs, and so on.

But the main problems in the traction field were, first, which system of electrification to adopt in future, and which main line project should have priority; and, second, how, quickly, to gain sufficient experience with diesel main line locomotives to enable bulk orders to be placed. In March 1956 the Commission announced that 25kV 50 Hz would be the future standard, except in the Southern Region. Important factors in this decision were the economy in the distribution system's fixed costs through much wider spacing of sub-stations, and reduction in the weight of the catenary support system and in the cost and weight of the copper conductor wire itself. This was because the high voltage system, for a given power, draws in inverse proportion a lower current, thus allowing conductors of much smaller cross section than would be needed for a comparable 1,500V dc network. An adverse factor was the need to provide increased clearance space between the live wire and any overhead structures, involving the lifting of many over-bridges.

It was argued that the reduction in cost of fixed installations on long stretches in open country outweighed the extra costs involved in built-up areas. This being the case, it seemed rather less than logical to convert the 1,500V dc line from Liverpool Street to Chelmsford, only completed in 1956, as well as the London, Tilbury & Southend line already in process of electrification at 1,500V, to the ac system at considerable cost. These systems were isolated from the rest of the country; even if the Great Eastern main had been joined later to an ac electrified system, the provision of dual-voltage locomotives 25kV ac and 1,500V dc would have presented no technical difficulty whatever. In short, for a number of years the new standard system was installed under precisely those circumstances where its special advantages could least be realised.

Its adoption led to a decision to install it on the eight miles of the Styal loop of the Manchester-Crewe line, as a pilot scheme. This was followed by complete electrification from Manchester to Crewe, then Crewe to Liverpool, the logic of which was not obvious until it could be followed by Euston-Crewe, both via the Trent Valley line and via Birmingham. This number of bites at the cherry annoyed the Ministry of Transport, which criticised the way in which extended commitments were being incurred without an overall scheme based on clear financial justification, and a comparison between the expected results from electrification and those from a changeover to diesel traction. This produced a long and unsatisfactory correspondence between the Region, the Commission and the Ministry. The Ministry never quite shook off the feeling that it had been pushed into authorising a huge scheme before receiving satisfactory answers to all the questions it had raised. The Minister's approval to completion of the LMR scheme was in fact withheld until January 1961, although electric operation (both locomotive-hauled and multiple-unit) between Manchester and Crewe had actually started in September 1960! Moreover the Minister himself,

Ernest Marples, had personally performed the formal opening ceremony.

In the event, of course, the London-Birmingham-Liverpool-Manchester electrification has fully justified itself; and inflation has written down its capital cost so effectively that it would have been tragic had it not been carried out.

But the peculiar way in which electrification crept ahead on the LMR put paid to the Eastern Region's main line project which, as early as 1951, had been recommended by the Harrington Committee as a first priority. Shortage of investment allocations as well as of Regional technical resources, prevented the GN main line scheme from getting off the ground quickly enough. The East Coast route did derive some comfort from the arrival in 1960-61 of the 22 English Electric 'Deltic' locomotives of 3,300hp which, with their 100mph capability with the heaviest trains, to some extent pre-empted the huge improvement in express train speeds on the LMR from electrification a few years later.

The London Midland Region's electrification involved a vast programme of physical works, including the reconstruction of such major stations as Euston, Birmingham (New Street), Manchester (Piccadilly, renamed from London Road), Coventry and Stafford. These works involved speed restrictions and track possessions on the main lines adversely affecting both train frequency and journey times. Alleviation was sought by concentrating much London-Manchester traffic on the Midland route from St Pancras, and London-Birmingham traffic upon the Paddington route.

A foretaste of things to come was the introduction of the 'Blue Pullmans'. These originated in the fertile brain of H.P. Barker, a part-time member of the BTC, who argued strenuously for the introduction on BR of high-speed diesel multiple-unit trains, of luxury character, for prime business services, akin to the Trans-Europ-Express trains being developed on the Continent at this period to compete with international air travel. A combination of the Pullman principle of meals at every seat and a high level of personal service, with multiple-

Above: The best-looking of the standard types? No 73014 at Bristol (Temple Meads) in 1956. (*C.R.L. Coles*). *Below:* The Ugly Duckling of the BR standard steam types? No 78046 at Riccarton Junction in 1956. (*I.S. Carr*)

Above: Before Beeching! A Buntingford branch train leaves St Margarets on probably the most rural branch line within 30 miles of London, about 1955. (*British Rail*). *Below:* BR tried to cut branch line costs with diesel traction; in the early 1950s this experimental ACV three-car railbus unit was used on a number of branches to assess its potential, including the Harrow–Belmont service seen here. (*G.M. Kichenside*)

unit construction allowing quick turn-round and high stock utilisation, was an attractive idea; and the Commission set up a small team — of which I was one — to exploit it.

Oddly enough, the Regions were not enthusiastic about the proposal, though the Western agreed that London-South Wales and London-Birmingham were routes upon which a prestige service of this type could be justified. The London Midland however — which one would have expected to welcome it in view of the adverse effect electrification works were bound to have on the Euston route — at first maintained that the only train paths available for the new service would be a daily trip from Derby to St Pancras and back!

This outraged common-sense. Our committee had as secretary a very able young man (a future BR Chief Passenger Manager) who had recently joined us from London Transport, Peter Keen. He took the LMR working timetable home with him and when he attended the next meeting was able to demonstrate convincingly the ability to find train paths from Manchester to London at a suitable morning hour and return in the evening, to which later was added a fill-in return trip from St Pancras to Leicester, later also to Nottingham, in the middle of the day.

The Blue Pullmans were intended to pioneer a new type of inter-city service. The concept was excellent in many ways but the realisation led to two troubles. Speeds were high, as predicted, the meal service was good and, for a time, the trains were popular with the businessmen who used them. But despite the use of the Schlieren bogie (which gave an excellent ride under lightweight coaches in its native Switzerland) the bad riding and some vibration from the motors caused unfavourable comparisons to be made with locomotive-hauled stock; for this and other reasons these trains had a relatively short life. And their introduction on routes over which Pullman services had not previously existed led to a major row with the National Union of Railwaymen. The BTC wanted the Pullman Company to work on the trains looking after the catering and personal service needs. The Pullman

Company's agreement with the Union was slightly less favourable to the men than that applying to BTC restaurant car staff. The London Midland men objected to a new service being staffed by Pullman and claimed the right to the jobs. In the end, the Pullman agreement was modified and the LMR men were taken on under the Pullman banner.

This episode however marked the beginning of the end for the Pullman Company, as a small, tightly-knit and efficient unit with its own traditions and management policy. The Company was eventually wound up, and its vehicles disposed of. Attempts to preserve the goodwill in the name gradually flickered out, the last remaining vestige being the 'Manchester Pullman' of the 1970s that was scarcely distinguishable from the other Inter-City electric expresses between Manchester and London.

The implementation of the Plan ran into heavy weather on a number of counts. Matters were not made easy by the need, on the one hand, to pay regard to Regional views, and on the other, the desire of the technical officers at headquarters to see standardisation for reasons of economy and efficiency. Then the views of the railway Central Staff and those of the Commission's General Staff did not always agree. Sir Brian had brought in as the head of the General Staff, with the designation of Secretary-General, an able Army administrator, Major-General Llewellyn Wansbrough-Jones. 'Wansbrough' as he was universally known, had been a Chief of Staff to General Montgomery and was skilled at sorting out differences and presenting a well-reasoned 'position paper'. But his exalted position vis-à-vis the railway managements gave rise to some tensions which, out of respect for Sir Brian, were always kept under control.

Acute problems arose over the introduction of diesel main line locomotives. The initial decision was to order 174 locomotives, 160 with electric transmission and 14 as diesel-hydraulics. Oddly enough, most were in the lower power ranges, up to 1,250hp; only 20 were to be of 2,000hp or over. Contracts were placed with a number of suppliers while the

BR workshops were in some case (not all) involved in manufacture of main frames, bogies and bodywork. An excessive number of types emerged. In 1957 the Chief Mechanical Engineer of BR gave the Commission a report on the desirability of narrowing the range of future orders: it listed seven engine types, eight forms of transmission and seven designers of the mechanical parts which were already in service. This failed to achieve its object; the Western Region successfully argued that hydraulic transmission should be used in the locomotives to be ordered for its services, leading to proliferation of the 1,700hp Hymek and the 2,700hp Maybach-Voith designs, built, as E.S. Cox has related, without prototype testing. Matters were not made easier for the Commission, committed as it was to allowing some degree of Regional independence, by the unease among the headquarters technical officers at the Western Region's vehement desire to be different and the contrary views expressed by Dr den Hollander, architect of the post-war reconstruction of the Netherlands Railways. He was regarded as one of the greatest European railwaymen of his day, and Sir Brian Robertson had invited him to join the Commission's Technical Development and Research Committee which he assisted until 1959. Dr den Hollander, perhaps partly from motives of Dutch patriotism, had no use for German practices among which he included hydraulic transmission. So, in an atmosphere of controversy, the original 174 prototypes for testing grew and grew, and the BTC seemed unable to shape any firm diesel policy.

Apart from traction, the Modernisation Plan ran into deep water on the freight side. About the same time as the Commission had decided to adopt 25kV ac electrification — accepting the immediate additional costs, including those of a changeover, in the prospect of ultimate technical gain — it took a decision, on precisely contrary grounds, to standardise the vacuum brake for freight wagons in preference to the air brake. The deciding factor had been the objection of the Regional General Managers to the inconvenience of a changeover, despite the arguments of the BR Central Staff for the air brake on technical grounds.

The decision that all wagons must in future be power braked was supported by what seemed unassailable logic. Operations would be vastly speeded up and the traditional brake van at the tail of the train could be dispensed with. Damage in transit from buffing shocks would be reduced, and another bonus would be the elimination of catch points on gradients designed to derail a runaway, saving on maintenance and signalling and track costs.

Yet when long and heavy mineral trains were fitted with the vacuum brake there were difficulties in starting and in releasing the brake after application. It was clear that the air brake would have been the right solution. But the total cost of fitting power brakes was enormous and in view of the limited life-expectancy of such a large proportion of the wagon fleet it could not be justified. Complete elimination of hand-braked wagons therefore had to be postponed. In fact, more and more merchandise wagons were power-brake fitted as time went on. But so long as *any* unbraked wagons were included in a train, the main advantages envisaged in the Modernisation Plan could not be realised, though some improvement was realised through the operation of trains with a 'fitted head' — ie a number of braked wagons at the front of the train coupled together and adding to the brake power provided by the locomotive.

In 1957/58 a team of BR officers, including A.J. White, Assistant General Manager of the Eastern Region, visited the United States in search of new developments possibly relevant to BR. They brought back one concept that seemed to have distinct possibilities — the 'Road-railer' designed for the Chesapeake & Ohio RR. It consisted of wagons very similar to the trailer portion of an articulated lorry, each with a single axle and supported at the front end by the preceding vehicle, rather like the 'Talgo' train in Spain, but designed with changeover wheelsets that enabled the wagons to run as a train with flanged steel wheels on rails, and when uncoupled and attached to a road tractor, to run on rubber-tyred road wheels. The change from one set to the other was performed by compressed air, a portable compresser being kept at, or brought to, any required point. A British version of this vehicle was built, having a payload of 11 tons and a tare weight of 5 tons.

The attraction was of course the ability to perform road collection and delivery services and also realise the speed and economy of train movement, without the transhipment of goods which added so much to costs, to delays and to the possibility of damage. An experimental BR train was sent on a tour and high hopes were placed on it. Unfortunately the project was found to have many drawbacks. The time taken to assemble the trains, or to break them up, was excessive and the system was so specialised that it needed regular and substantial flows of traffic between fixed points. In the event, it was superseded by the Freightliner concept. But it was an interesting example of the numerous attempts that have been made to design a true road-rail vehicle, sometimes quite successfully in the technical sense but nearly always operationally or economically unsatisfactory. The LMS had a passenger vehicle of this kind in John Shearman's 'Ro-Railer' of 1931, and such vehicles were used for a long time by the District Engineers for track maintenance purposes in the remoter parts of Scotland, where their ability to transport men and materials to a working site could be greatly increased by using either rail or road as most convenient.

The marshalling yard national plan fell into deep trouble, because of the decline in total tonnage, and the changes in the traffic flows which overtook the railways even while the new yards were under construction, so that most of them never achieved the wagon throughput for which they were designed.

Steering the execution of the Modernisation Plan through these troubled waters was difficult because each Area Board pressed very strongly for a maximum slice of the investment cake. The technical officers in the BR Central Staff pleaded for a single overall plan and, in the interests of economy and efficiency, for a very limited number of designs for traction and rolling stock. The Commission received these points of view filtered through the General Staff, composed of Advisers — covering the fields of Traffic, Manpower, Technical, Supplies and Production and Public Relations — presided over by the Secretary-General. The first S-G had been General Sir Daril Watson. When he retired and was followed by Major-General Llewellyn Wansbrough-Jones, this gave rise to a certain amount of comment about the military style of the BTC headquarters. It certainly was the case that a marked change took place in the form of the Commission's Annual Reports. Under Sir Cyril (Lord) Hurcomb as an ex-Civil Servant these had devoted much space to a section headed 'Progress Towards the Objectives of the Transport Act'. Now the emphasis was all on resources for execution of what was conceived to be the Commission's objective: Manpower: Development: Finance. Commercial policy was not prominent.

Unhappily, despite the injection of investment under the Modernisation Plan, the railway position worsened. Net receipts, in the years after the Plan was launched, disappeared and were replaced by a deficit of £16.5 million in 1956, growing in successive years to £27.1 million, £48.1 million and finally in 1959 only slightly improving to £42 million. If to these working results there were added the estimated liability for the railway share of the BTC's central charges — mainly administration and interest on loans — there were notional 'railway' deficits of £68.1 million in 1957 £90.1 million in 1958 and £84 million in 1959.

These results caused the Government great concern. The concern was shared by Parliament; and the House of Commons Select Committee on the Nationalised Industries carried out a lengthy study of British Railways published in July 1960. The Committee concluded that the losses were mainly incurred by BR's passenger services and above all by the stopping trains on branches and lightly-used services, but they suspected that losses were diffused through the system and in their Report remarked rather acidly 'The more important point is that the

Commission cannot say with any precision where this £42 million [deficit in 1959] is lost'.

The Committee also had some hard things to say about the Modernisation Plan. The Plan's cost had been 're-appraised' by the BTC's General Staff in 1957 and rose to £1,500 million. In view of the fall in railway receipts, the Commission had reviewed the Plan for the benefit of the Ministry of Transport. The Committee commented: 'for the first time, the Ministry became aware of the way in which the Commission's figures had been calculated. What they learnt came as a shock. It was apparent that the anticipated return on new investment was not as attractive as, in general terms, it had seemed to be'.

Now in 1960, acceptance of the principle of comparability of railway wages with those in other nationalised industries, the public service and appropriate private businesses, led to a serious financial problem. The comparability studies had been made by Mr C.W. Guillebaud and led to claims for substantial pay rises. The Government broadly accepted the Guillebaud report and consequent agreements with the unions led to a major increase in railway costs. The Select Committee commented that this had 'brought the Commission's financial crisis to a head'.

The Committee summed up their conclusions on two major points. They thought that the BTC should *not* have spent money on providing 'social' services, which did not cover their costs: 'this confusion in judging between what is economically right and what is socially desirable has played an important part in leading to the situation in which the Commission now find themselves.' But all was not lost! The Committee continued: 'On the evidence they have received, there is no doubt that a large-scale British railway system can be profitable .... What size and shape should British Railways be? The first consideration must be financial.'

The patient's symptoms had now been described. The doctor was to be summoned for diagnosis and treatment.

Chapter 13
The Doctor's Dilemma

When the railways came under the microscope of the House of Commons Select Committee, they escaped without any very drastic recommendations for reform or reorganisation. The Committee had received much evidence from Sir Brian Robertson, and in their Report said that they had 'been greatly impressed by the evidence given, with a most distinguished breadth of mind and clarity of expression, by the Chairman of the Commission'. It was in fact difficult not to be impressed by Sir Brian, whether you thought he was always right or not.

But a less flattering picture seems to have been painted by a small Special Advisory Group appointed about the same time by the Minister of Transport, Ernest Marples, to advise him about the worsening situation of BR. This group, chaired by an industrialist, Sir Ivan Stedeford, worked in private and its written report or reports to Mr Marples have never been made available to historians by the Ministry. But subsequent events indicate that they were strongly critical both of the Commission's organisation and of its policies. On the organisation side, there was certainly an anomaly. The Commission on the one hand presided, rather like a holding company controlling subsidiary companies, over a group of widely different businesses, mostly with their own chief executives — London Transport, British Road Services, British Transport Docks, British Waterways, British Transport Hotels — not to mention the bus groups or Thomas Cook & Son. But on the other hand the Commission was itself the only central management or chief executive for the railways, co-ordinating and controlling the six Area Boards and the Regional managements.

The Stedeford group, like the Select Committee, seem to

have thought that the railways could and should be run as a commercially profitable undertaking, if only the top management would shake off its 'public service' mentality. It needed, in short, to be directed by businessmen and (by implication) even a highly distinguished public servant like Sir Brian was not the ideal Chairman, because of his training and background. The solution was therefore to break up the huge unwieldy Commission and put the railways under a Board directly responsbile to the Minister — a Board moreover that would be commercially motivated.

It happened that a member of the Stedeford group who had greatly impressed the Minister was Dr Richard Beeching, Technical Director of Imperial Chemical Industries Ltd. He struck Mr Marples as being just the man who was needed to bring the necessary business outlook to the railways. Sir Brian Robertson was retiring at the end of May 1961 and this opened the way for what was to become known as the Beeching era on BR.

Dr Beeching's personality differed considerably from that of Sir Brian Robertson. Sir Brian saw the railways as primarily a public service which it was his duty to provide, subject to guidance from political masters. Having created an administrative machine, he expected everyone involved in it to carry out their appointed tasks. He expected his own integrity and loyalty to be reciprocated by his subordinates, but he did not demand from them more than competence and loyalty. He was prepared to accept all responsibility for decision-making; as he told the Select Committee, he himself and not the BTC's Secretary-General must be regarded as the chief executive. In other words, it was something of a military approach.

The Press indeed used to refer to 'BR's Generals' though in fact there was never more than a handful, scattered throughout the BTC and its businesses. Elsewhere I have written (in *Modern Railways*) that Sir Brian's appearance 'was austere and formidable; he was prone to prolonged silences which sometimes created near-panic among young railway officers who had to entertain him on inspection tours. But his officers soon discovered that he had a clear and logical mind; if he was stiff with them, he could unbend and talk more easily with the "other ranks". His silences came more from shyness than dislike of his fellow-men; he was capable of kindnesses and showed sincere distress at the death of a staunch and loyal colleague.'

Dr Beeching created a very different atmosphere. He was relaxed and courteous, one might say friendly, smoking expensive cigars. But he quickly showed that he had a formidable intellect as well as a wonderful capacity for lucid exposition of a complicated issue. He was not interested in formal patterns of organisation, much more with setting the scene so that people could act sensibly within it. He allowed Robertson's complicated structure of General Staff, Central Staff, Sub-Commissions and Committees to wither away by simply omitting to summon meetings of bodies which appeared unnecessary. He preferred to assign jobs and functions to Board Members according to his estimate of their capacities, rather than some organisation chart. It is sometimes forgotten how short in fact Dr Beeching's period in office was — only four years — because of the deep impression made by the changes effected under his leadership.

But it is perhaps worth while, before looking at the 'Beeching Re-shaping', to review briefly what was happening in the physical state of the railways. The fruits of the Modernisation Plan were beginning to be gathered by the end of 1962. Diesel locomotives increased in number from 452 (mostly shunters) in 1955 to 3,179. Electrification schemes that had been in the pipeline (to mix a metaphor!) before the Plan were beginning to come into operation. In 1956 the Liverpool Street-Chelmsford and Southend (Victoria) sections had opened at 1,500V dc; in 1959 the Colchester-Clacton-Walton 25kV ac section followed, as did the first phase of the Southern Region's 750V dc third rail Kent Coast electrification from Gillingham to Ramsgate, Sheerness and Dover. By 1960 the tempo of electrification was quickening. In that year the Crewe-Manchester section came into service, as did the first phase of the Glasgow suburban electrification, covering 52 track miles on the North side of the Clyde. In November of the same year, services started on the whole 'Chenford' scheme — Liverpool Street to Enfield Town, Chingford, Hertford and Bishop's Stortford. The following year saw completion of the conversion of the Liverpool Street electrified lines to 25kV ac traction.

The inauguration of the electrified lines did not always take place smoothly. Immediately after the Glasgow routes, served by attractively designed 'Blue Trains', opened for public service there were some alarming instances of fires in the electric traction equipment on the trains and there had to be a sudden reversion to steam haulage until the faults could be rectified by the manufacturers of the equipment. Other troubles developed in the rolling stock working over the 'Chenford' network, which also had to be withdrawn for modification by the suppliers of the equipment, though in this case it was possible to operate temporarily a restricted service using some of the trains built for the London, Tilbury & Southend line which had not yet come into operation.

By 1962 the second stage of the Euston main line electrification was completed, with conversion of the Crewe-Liverpool section. The second phase of the Southern's Kent Coast electrification was also finished, covering Sevenoaks-Tonbridge-Dover-Deal-Ramsgate and branches, 132 route miles in all. In the same year the Glasgow suburban lines south of the Clyde (Glasgow Central to Cathcart, Neilston, Kirkhill and Motherwell) started electric operation. And at last, the electrification project that had in fact been the first to be studied and agreed after nationalisation, the London, Tilbury and Southend system, saw the introduction of full electric services and the complete withdrawal of steam in June 1962.

Diesel services were increasing steadily also; the arrival of the 'Deltics' on the East Coast Main Line in 1961 led to considerable accelerations between King's Cross, Newcastle and Leeds.

The Southern had made considerable progress towards elimination of steam traction in the areas originally proposed in the Southern Railway's report of February 1946. In 1957 diesel-electric main line corridor multiple-units had replaced steam on the Charing Cross and Cannon Street services to Hastings via Tunbridge Wells, and about the same time, there was an extensive substitution of steam stopping trains in the Hampshire area by local diesel-electric multiple-units, similar in many ways to standard Southern suburban emus apart from the diesel motor and generator in the power compartment.

Other aspects of the Modernisation Plan were less successful. It was nearly 1960 before work began on the new marshalling yard at Carlisle — a project that was to take 2½ years to completion — at a time when freight traffic was falling ominously from 274 million tons originating in 1955 to 249 million in 1960. In the same five years the total number of road goods vehicles in use had risen from 1.1 million to 1.4 million; registration of new goods vehicles had been 154,000 in the year 1955, but 226,100 in 1960.

It was against this background of a substantial flow of technical improvements in the railway service, but worsening financial results, that the Conservative Government decided upon fairly drastic measures. These were described in a White Paper dated December 1960 and entitled 'Reorganisation of the Nationalised Transport Undertakings'. The Government, the paper said, in reaching their conclusions had been assisted by the advice given by the Stedeford group.

The White Paper argued that the heart of the BTC's problem was the railways. 'The activities of the British Transport Commission as at present constituted are so large and so diverse that it is virtually impossible to run them effectively as a single undertaking'. So it was proposed to break up the Commission, ending the vast experiment that had started in 1948, putting the railways under a British Railways Board appointed by the Minister, with Regional Railway Boards replacing the Area Boards of the BTC. The other parts of the Commission's undertaking were also to come under new Boards (and a Transport Holding Company) directly answering to the Minister.

The Transport Act, 1962, giving effect to these proposals, came into force in September of that year and as from 1 January 1963 the BRB replaced the BTC as the governing body of the railways.

Meanwhile Dr Beeching had held a Press conference at which he said 'Losses may even get worse before they get better . . . . doubts about the future of the railway system as a whole can only be resolved by a more thoroughgoing study of the present working and future prospects of the system than has been made so far'. By the end of 1961 these studies were well in hand, steered at BTC headquarters by S.E. (later Sir Stanley) Raymond, then Traffic Adviser.

The aim of the studies was simple; to find out which traffics were carried at a profit and which at a loss; which parts of the system were commercially viable and which were only maintained through subsidy. Underlying them was the idea that by discarding the unprofitable traffics and closing the non-viable portions of the system, the remainder must come into economic health, assuming that it received enough investment to develop all potentially profitable activities.

The core of the studies was the traffic analyses which of course had to be carried out by the Regions, but which were collated and digested at headquarters, with results displayed in maps and diagrams in a kind of Operations Room. There was pressure to reach conclusions quickly which meant that the extent of investigations in detail had to be restricted to a single traffic density survey over all lines, followed by very extensive use of statistics already available in Regional offices, which in some cases had to substitute averages for ascertained actual figures. The surveys, however, bringing together — often for the first time — receipts and outgoings for particular types of traffic and particular sections of line, yielded some startling disclosures. These were given to the world in what has since become known as the 'Beeching Report', though its actual title is *The Reshaping of British Railways*.

The Report was written with a clarity (it was in fact mainly drafted by Beeching himself) that made its logic seem irresistible. Even to-day it still reads well. It began by recalling that the Prime Minister, Mr Harold Macmillan, had said in Parliament in March 1960 that 'the railway system must be remodelled to meet current needs'. But the Report did not assume that simple surgery would be appropriate; it emphasised 'that the proposals now made are not directed towards achieving that result [making the railways pay] by the simple and unsatisfactory method of rejecting all those parts of the system which do not pay already or which cannot be made to pay easily .... proposals are directed towards developing to the full those parts of the system and those services which can be made to meet traffic requirements more efficiently and satisfactorily than any alternative form of transport, and towards eliminating only those services which, by their very nature, railways are ill-suited to provide'.

These cautious words were however largely ignored by the public during the furore created by the revelations in the Report. These included the news that BR had some 7,000 stations of which half produced only two per cent of the total traffic. A quarter of the total receipts originated at 34 stations only.

Turning from stations as generators of traffic to the lines over which the traffic was carried, the Report showed that one-third of the mileage carried only one per cent of the traffic, expressed in ton-miles and passenger-miles. One half of the system did not carry traffic sufficient to maintain the track and structures, let alone contribute anything towards the cost of movement.

Utilisation was not only poor as regards fixed assets; the average annual weekly mileage per wagon in the stock was pathetically low at 45 miles of revenue-earning work. Passenger rolling stock was excessive for the work load. Out of 18,500 main line type carriages, only 5,500 were in all-year-round service, the remainder being used only for summer or high peak services, or else being under or awaiting repair. Stopping passenger services as a group failed to cover even their direct movement costs, while London's commuter services yielded no profit margin adequate to justify new investment that was badly needed. Wagon-load freight as a class was very unprofitable, as were 'sundries' or small consignments, though train-load freight could be profitable.

But public attention was focussed on the long list of stations in an Appendix to the Report — some 2000 — and list of train services — around 250 — which, on purely economic grounds, it was suggested should be closed or withdrawn.

There was something of a *succès de scandale* over this document; it made Dr Beeching a national figure almost overnight, and a bogey-man to some. However, he applied his great powers of exposition to explaining the logic of his proposals through the media. In many ways he was a great contrast to his predecessor, although Sir Brian was also a master of clear exposition in the military manner. (In fact, when he had unfolded his ineffably complex headquarters organisation for the BTC to the officers, he had received a spontaneous outburst of applause for a masterly presentation.) But Dr Beeching did not lecture; in a more relaxed way, he discussed the problem and indicated the logical answer, as he saw it. His political masters gave him full support against the outcry that the reshaping proposals inevitably provoked among rail users and the railway unions.

Not enough attention was paid by the Press and the public to the positive side of the 'Reshaping' report, particularly Appendix 4 describing the 'Liner Train' concept of 'transport based upon joint use of road and rail for door-to-door transport of containerised merchandise, with special-purpose, through-running, scheduled trains providing the trunk haul'. This was the forerunner of the Freightliner service, one day to be described as the brightest jewel in BR's crown.

Unfortunately, although the report showed where losses were being incurred, it did not follow that discontinuance of such services or closures of such sections of line would enable equivalent savings to be made. There were many complicating factors: the loss of 'contributory value' from through transits, only part of which might be uneconomic; delays in realising staff reductions through redundancy agreements and the filling of vacancies by displaced personnel; the costs of providing alternative facilities and of making safe abandoned assets. Moreover the Transport Users' Consultative Committees created as customer watchdogs by the Transport Act, 1947, despite having had their scope curtailed under the 1962 Act, still had to consider every case for the complete withdrawal of passenger services from any station or on any line, from the angle of the anticipated hardship to users.

The list of closures submitted to the TUCCs of course grew rapidly after publication of the Reshaping report and by the end of 1963 a total of 167 proposals for line closures had been published. The machine had begun to grind. Looking ahead, the result of the accelerated programme of closures denominated as re-shaping may be summarised as follows: route-miles open for traffic had been 18,214 at the end of 1961; at the end of 1969, there were 12,098. Total stations in 1961 had been 7,025; in 1969 there were 3,002.

The process of reshaping, like that of the Modernisation Plan, did not start on a given date and end on another. It merely speeded up and gave coherence to a process that was already at work.

Before Dr Beeching's arrival I had been Chairman of the Unremunerative Services Committee in the Eastern Region and, using traffic density statistics similar to those later used in the Reshaping report, had produced a map entitled 'The Economic Region'. Lines which, on traffic densities, were almost certainly uneconomic were distinguished from the viable portions of the system.

The map was shown to the Chairman of the Area Board, Sir Reginald Wilson. His first reaction was to welcome it as a valuable guide to policy; his second, to give a directive that it was to be locked up and kept strictly confidential! He was of course absolutely right. Premature disclosure of the map would have led to traders hastening to transfer their traffic to road, fearing the loss of rail freight facilities, and to vociferous agitation by communities against the withdrawal of passenger

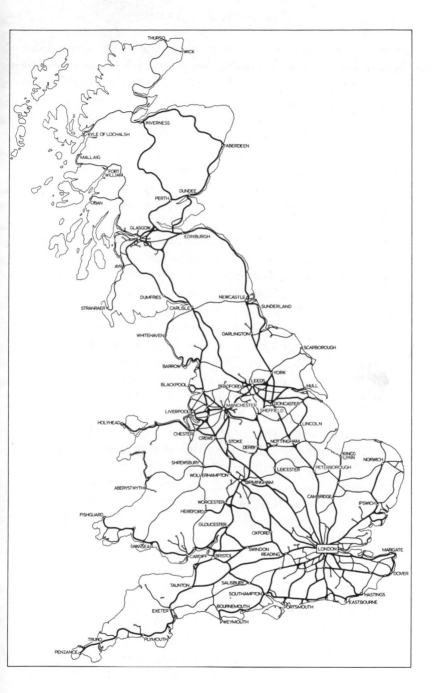

BRF25Y H

services. I did manage to obtain permission for copies of the map to be supplied to District Engineers (though to be kept under lock and key) in order that no major expenditure should be incurred without the General Manager's express authority on those lines whose economics were bad. As a rider to this, it was a demand from the Civil Engineer for immediate authority to reconstruct (at very substantial expense) a major bridge on the Midland & Great Northern Joint Line that led to my being instructed to prepare urgently the case for closure of that system, which was estimated to lose about £640,000 a year.

The dilemma which Sir Reginald Wilson solved by keeping the cards very close to his chest, and by Dr Beeching in the opposite way by publishing, and demanding support for his logic, was very real. It was not necessarily the case that inside a large unprofitable railway there was a small profitable railway struggling to get out. The interdependence of the parts of the network was far greater than the rather crude, generalised statistics of the Reshaping Report could show.

Dr Beeching was more aware of this than his Press and public critics realised. It is too often forgotten that the Reshaping report was followed by 'The Development of the Major Trunk Routes', a survey of how traffic could be concentrated and how investment could be justified, on the main lines. The Beeching philosophy in fact was not merely one of contraction but one of concentration upon those tasks for which railways are technically best qualified. It was not really new: it had been outlined as long ago as 1949 by the BTC in its Annual Report for that year but from both internal and external causes — management problems and political changes — had never been implemented. Could it have been, while road-rail integration was still a possibility, the whole history of British transport might have been different. In fact Dr Beeching should, ideally, have produced his 'Reshaping' report a decade and a half earlier. But when he retired in 1965 he could claim that, if he had not made British Railways pay its way, at least he had contained the deficit despite steadily increasing wage levels. The Annual Report for 1963 contained a section entitled 'Towards a Modern Railway', which recited how the fruits of the Modernisation Plan of 1955 were being combined with the positive elements in the Reshaping plan. Freightliner trains had started to run between Glasgow and London; 'Merry-go-round' block trains of coal between pitheads and power stations were about to start operations, and the electrification programme was being extended to cover the route from Glasgow to Gourock and Wemyss Bay, and the Southern Region main line to Southampton and Bournemouth. The decade of really intensive changes had got well under way.

Chapter 14

Mrs Castle's New Railway

In October 1964 the General Election returned a Labour Government to power, and it was too much to expect a Labour Minister of Transport to smile benevolently upon the policy which Ernest Marples had inaugurated and Dr Beeching was carrying through. A new look at transport was inevitable, and preliminary discussions between the Minister, Mrs Barbara Castle, and Dr Beeching revealed that there was a wide difference of opinion as to the direction in which future policy for the railways should proceed.

Dr Beeching therefore decided to return to Imperial Chemical Industries; he relinquished the Chairmanship on 31 May 1965 and in the Birthday Honours received a peerage. He was succeeded by S.E. Raymond, who had master-minded the traffic surveys for the Reshaping report and subsequently became a Vice-Chairman of the Board. In a short farewell talk to the chief officers Dr Beeching asked them to give Raymond particular support, because — as he put it — while he had enjoyed a special relationship with, and support from, his Minister, this was not necessarily going to be the case with his successor. How prophetic these words were to prove, no more than 31 months later, he could not have foreseen.

Raymond (who became Sir Stanley in 1966) had, unlike Beeching, long personal connections with prominent figures in the Labour Party. He was proud of the fact that he had come from an orphanage and fought his way to the top, first as a trade union organiser, then as a personnel expert in London Transport, a manager with British Road Services, Assistant General Manager of BR's Scottish Region, General Manager of the Western Region, finally attaining Board status. His deep, almost emotional involvement in policy issues was in contrast to his predecessor's calm and analytical approach. His capacity for work was prodigious, and this sometimes led him to take on tasks that could well have been left to others. His reputation for impatience and ruthlessness covered a real dedication to the job and considerable inner sensitivity.

A particular hot potato which Raymond picked up was the amalgamation of the Eastern and North Eastern Regions, decided upon by the BRB in December 1965. It proved highly controversial and inevitably caused much concern to the staff concerned. The unions objected strongly and pressed their point with the Minister, Mrs Castle. Finally the Minister's approval was given in November 1966 and the merger began to take effect at the beginning of 1967, no less than two years thereafter being required to complete the transfer of staff and the full reorganisation. The new Regional headquarters became York, a distant location from which to oversee, for instance, the electrification of the King's Cross suburban lines or the commuter traffic of Liverpool Street.

By 1966 the new Government had begun to form some ideas about what needed to be done, and issued a White Paper 'Transport Policy' which promised to give the British Railways Board more realistic financial objectives and a new financial framework, with closer integration of public sector road and rail services. It indicated that the heavy losses which the railways were incurring over passenger services provided for 'social reasons' would be met from specific grants.

But of course there could be no question of a blank cheque being given to the BRB. A Joint Steering Group was set up to report jointly to the Minister and the BRB Chairman. It was composed of representatives of BR, the Ministry of Transport, other Government departments, and outside experts. Its task was to examine just where losses were being made, and to look also at the 'standby' element in railway infra-structure costs — the burden of keeping a transport framework going to meet any possible future national need. It also looked at the railway organisation.

So once again BR came under the microscope while civil

servants and advisers within the Ministry of Transport began drafting a new Transport Act. Rather plaintively, the Board complained in the Annual Report for 1966 that 'the Board will probably have to operate for another two years on the existing financial basis. It is not good for the morale of the staff or for a proper understanding of the problem by the public that British Railways should continue for so long on this basis'.

'This basis' consisted of annual deficits estimated to be around £130 million. In fact, the deficit for 1967 rose to £153 million. At the same time, the new railway was emerging in the form of main line electrification, Freightliner services, 100-ton oil tank wagons and new Mark II coaching stock.

At last the Government's detailed proposals were revealed. A team of economists had assisted or supplemented the work of the civil servants in the Ministry of Transport and full account was taken of the detailed studies of the Joint Steering Group.

No less than three White Papers foreshadowing legislation came out in 1967 — 'Railway Policy' and 'Transport of Freight' in November, and 'Public Transport and Traffic' in December. It was ironical that Sir Stanley Raymond should not have remained to see the legislation brought into force. He had disagreed so strongly with Mrs Castle over part of her proposals that it was impossible for him to continue in office, which he had to relinquish abruptly on 31 December 1967. Yet with most of the proposals emanating from the work of the Joint Steering Group he must have been in agreement.

The Transport Act, 1968, when passed, was a mammoth statute, containing 166 Sections and 18 Schedules, 281 pages of print — even longer than the original nationalisation Act of 1947. The solution to BR's problems was set out in three main parts. First of all, a large part of the capital debt would be written off. Next, there would be a complete separation of the 'commercial' from the 'social' passenger train services. The latter would be grant-aided for as long as the Minister required them to continue. Then, on the freight side, the loss-making sundries business would be removed from the railways and handed over — terminals, staff, and road collection and delivery vehicles — to a newly-created National Freight Corporation which also would be in charge of British Road Services.

The identification of the sundries business of small consignments, and its separation from the wagon-load and train-load freight business, had been put in hand by the BRB in anticipation of legislation, so that its constitution as a separate company owned by the National Freight Corporation could be smoothly arranged once the Act came into force.

Another major part of this immense Act was the constitution of Passenger Transport Executives in major conurbations, to some extent resembling London Transport, but under the control of Passenger Transport Authorities which in effect anticipated the creation of the Metropolitan Counties that later assumed control of the PTEs. The latter were empowered to enter into agreements with the railways for the operation of local train services, and to make payments for the maintenance of uneconomic services. The initial PTEs were in Merseyside, the West Midlands, Tyneside, and Greater Manchester.

Implicit in the Act was the replacement of reshaping by subsidy. Closures in fact virtually came to a halt; the route-mileage was 12,434 at the end of 1968 and four years later, at the end of 1972, had only fallen to 11,537.

The only part of the Act which the BRB found really hard to swallow was the handing over of control of the Freightliner Company to the National Freight Corporation. The railways retained a substantial minority interest — the split in fact was 51% NFC: 49% BRB — but having nursed this business into growth, and pinning great hopes on it for the future, there was resentment at seeing it placed under the NFC.

The most immediate effect of the Act was to enable the BRB to finish the year 1969 with a railway operating surplus of £48.5 millions, and an overall surplus, after bringing in the net receipts of the non-railway activities and meeting interest and other central charges, of £14.7 millions, a welcome change from the sad tale of deficits. This resulted from the inclusion of grants as income of its passenger business.

The Act also reflected the views of the Joint Steering Group about the organisation; it required the BRB to report to the Minister within 12 months with proposals for their future organisation. Looking ahead, the BRB employed consultants, McKinsey and Company Inc, to prepare a scheme in consultation with the BRB Chairman, Members and Chief Officers. By the end of 1969 a scheme had been submitted to and approved by the Minister. Its main feature was a distinction between the 'corporate' role of the Board, whose members should be mainly non-executive, and the railway and other businesses controlled by the BRB, each of which should be managed by a Chief Executive. Each of the 'other' businesses was to have a subsidiary Board of management, but the railways would continue to have Regional Railway Boards, although these were no longer to be statutory bodies, provision for them having disappeared from the 1968 Act.

The chief beneficiary of this much sunnier climate was the new Chairman, H.C. (Sir Henry) Johnson, who took over on 1 January 1968 after Raymond's abrupt and unexpected departure. His temperament was very different from that of his predecessor. A highly professional railwayman whose background was operating, he had been successively General Manager of the Eastern and London Midland Regions, and then a Vice-Chairman of the Board. He had throughout his career the wonderful instinct or knack of being the right man in the right place at the right time; now he presided over BR just when the financial position had been, at any rate for a few years, straightened out and when technical developments were greatly improving the quality of service. His period in office, which ended in September 1971, had in fact something of a honeymoon character and of course, like all honeymoons, was rather brief.

Chapter 15
The Decade of Change

The first years of the 1960s saw the re-shaping and its consequences; the later years saw the modern BR emerging, with main line electrification, the complete disappearance of steam traction, the new rolling stock liveries in which blue and grey predominated, the concept of 'Inter-City', and — sadly — the withering-away of the wagon-load freight traffic. The decade also saw the second attempt by a Labour Government to rationalise and rearrange public sector transport without reverting to the principles on which the 1948 BTC had been created. It also saw a massive reduction in the staff employed, and new job specifications designed to increase productivity.

Perhaps the most notable feature of the decade was the determined attempt to introduce more modern technology on the railways. At the end of the 1950s there was not really a vast amount of difference between BR and the pre-war companies; by the beginning of the 1970s there had been vast changes, with more on the way. As early as 1960 the BTC had decided that research must be rapidly expanded. Hitherto the railways had relied mainly upon the laboratories at Derby built in the 1930s by the LMS railway. Now they decided greatly to expand the facilities and attract more scientific staff, the cost being around £1¼ million. New chemical laboratories were built at Muswell Hill on the site of a closed station, and new building work at Derby went on through 1961 and 1962. The Research Department was reorganised in four Divisions — Chemical, Engineering, Electrical, and Regional Scientific Services; arrangements for technical collaboration with outside organisations were strengthened. These outside bodies included universities and research associations, the Locomotive and Allied Manufacturers' Association and the Research Organisation (ORE) of the International Union of Railways (UIC).

In May 1964 the Duke of Edinburgh opened the new Derby complex and the increase in research activity acquired great momentum. A major problem had arisen from a disturbing increase in wagon derailments, which appeared to be a consequence of the higher acceleration and speeds of freight traffic with diesel traction. It had led to the imposition for the time being of a 45mph speed limit on freight trains. There had also long been dissatisfaction with the riding of the bogies under Mark I passenger coaches. A palliative had been sought by the use of Commonwealth bogies with compound springing, but these were unduly heavy and expensive.

The Research Department concentrated much effort to studying vehicle riding and the behaviour of four-wheeled vehicles and bogies, and the effect of different suspension systems. In 1965 the BRB reported its concern that the fleet of short wheelbase four-wheel wagons could not be operated with complete safety at the higher speeds envisaged under modernisation, and its decision to intensify research into the basic dynamics of railway vehicles on the track. By 1967 it was able to announce that these studies had led to the concept of an Advanced Passenger Train, incorporating a body-tilting suspension system to minimise the centrifugal forces when rounding curves. The APT was subjected to prolonged and exhaustive testing at each stage, both in the laboratory and over a length of former main line allocated for high-speed test running, well into the 1970s. Apart from the tilting body, it incorporated a 'self-steering' bogie design and a novel 'hydro-kinetic' brake to permit rapid stopping from the high running speeds (155mph) envisaged.

The APT was to figure very largely in all BR planning, not merely into the 1970s but into the 1980s, before it entered 'squadron service'. The extended timescale was due to three principal factors. One was the insistence — very soundly based — that a project incorporating not one but several

130

technical innovations must be exhaustively tested at each stage of development. Another was that the original idea of a small gas turbine motive unit had to be abandoned — partly because the manufacturers, who had produced a prototype designed for heavy road vehicles decided to drop the project — in favour of electric traction, which posed new problems of current collection. A third was that APT involved a new system of rail transport, not just a new type of train. (See Chapter 25) And there was the continuing problem of persuading a sceptical or timid Ministry to allocate funds on a really adequate scale.

While APT was still in the early development stage, a substantial increment of practical modernisation was obtained from the opening throughout of the Euston-Birmingham-Liverpool-Manchester electrification in March 1967, while in October of the following year the new Euston station was opened by HM The Queen. The improvement in traffic receipts from the introduction of 100mph services was immediate.

It was not merely high speed but improved riding comfort that impressed the public. Dissatisfaction with the Mark I passenger stock, not merely its riding qualities but also its interior design, had led as early as 1957 to the production of 13 new prototype side corridor and open interior coaches of different designs, some from railway shops and some from private builders. It was the intention to move from the traditional underframe and body shell design to integral construction, but it was not until 1964 that new stock — christened XP64 — was put into trial service; even then it utilised Mark I underframes pending the change to integral construction.

XP64 was the forerunner of the Mark II series, ranging from 'a' to 'f', and progressing from only modest improvement on Mark I, to the later series that, with wide doors and full air-conditioning at last could stand comparison with the modern vehicles to be found on the Continent. But it was something of a tragedy — from the passenger marketing angle at least —

that for various reasons, the main one being the lack of a clear train catering policy, no new restaurant or buffet cars were ever built to Mark II designs. So the new electric expresses incorporated rough-riding, though 'face-lifted', Mark I catering vehicles. Even so, the London Midland Region electrics set much higher standards for fast and comfortable Inter-City travel in 1967. The term Inter-City in fact originated there — borrowed from a named Paddington-Birmingham express but obviously too good to waste on a single train. Now it is used as a brand name by several European railways as well!

In July of the same year the Southern Region inaugurated main line electric services between London, Southampton and Bournemouth, with on some services a novel combination of high-powered four-car electric multiple-units propelling one or two unpowered four-car units, taken on by diesel locomotive from Bournemouth to Weymouth.

The Bournemouth services had been just about the last upon which express passenger services were steam-hauled. In August 1968 the last standard-gauge British Railways steam train to run for many years was provided for enthusiasts on a special excursion trip from Liverpool to Carlisle and back. The only remaining BR steam locomotives in use became those on the (summer only) Aberystwyth-Devil's Bridge narrow-gauge tourist train service. So the whole process of eliminating steam had taken little more than 12 years from the first policy announcement in the Modernisation Plan.

For some years thereafter it seemed as though steam was, in the eyes of BR's higher management, identified with everything that was old-fashioned, inefficient and uncommercial. There was a complete ban on the use of BR metals by preservation societies or other bodies owning steam locomotives and anxious to organise steam enthusiasts' excursions. This was a symptom, not perhaps very important in itself, of a change of management style at the centre which was felt at all levels in the undertaking.

The Stedeford Group had recommended, it is reasonable to deduce, that BR should become more 'commercial' in outlook by importing managers from private industry. Invitations were in fact extended to a number of leading businesses to second or release managers to work in BR; there were Press advertisements (previously unheard-of in the railway world) for Regional Assistant General Manager posts.

The best-known of the imported figures was Philip H. Shirley, who became first a full-time Board Member and then a Vice-Chairman. Australian in origin, he had trained as an accountant with Peat Marwick and Mitchell and become the Chief Accountant of the Unilever Group and later Managing Director of one of their principal subsidiaries. Shirley became something of a legend on the railways because of his obsession with obtaining high utilisation of assets, whether infrastructure or traction and rolling stock, his searching, often at local stations or depots, for redundant assets such as little-used sidings, and his habit of sniffing out 'nonsenses' of the kind that lurk in the darker corners of every large undertaking. He was not therefore always welcomed as warmly as might have been the case on visits or inspections, though his often pungent comments could stimulate fresh thought and discussion on important issues.

At a slightly less exalted level, the 'old hands' decided that the quality of the new blood was variable. It would be an over-simplification to say that the new men came to scoff and remained to pray; but if they had expected to find railway managers fumbling with problems that only needed firm handling, they soon learnt that this was not so, and that the general level of competence among railwaymen was at least as high as in large-scale industry generally. The newcomers served their term and then mostly returned to their previous employment though one or two stayed on to make their future careers with BR.

There was however one consequence of the new style of 'business management' for which the 'Beeching boys' were largely responsible. This was a reaction against any concept of public service and even more against the idea that anyone could be in railways because they liked railways. That was 'playing trains' and it was supposed to have been a fault of past generations of railwaymen.

Those who could remember the commercial drive of an Ashton Davies on the LMS before the war, or the tough negotiations over rates between former Goods Managers and important traders, could reject the over-simplified idea that railways had ever been run for fun. But many of the younger officers felt that their promotion might depend upon their giving a tolerable imitation of a tough business tycoon. Those who had an interest in railway history, liked railways for their own sake, or who even (shamefully) owned an extensive model railway at home, felt it essential to hide these damaging facts from top management.

On the other side, the new men certainly brought some constructive ideas to bear. For instance, a determined drive was launched to obtain contracts for train load traffic, particularly oil; new contacts with the oil companies were all-important here. And, reversing the policy of getting rid of private owners wagons that had seemed so important just after nationalisation, large firms were persuaded to construct their own special-purpose wagons for bulk traffics. Philip Shirley was tireless in propaganda for the Freightliner system, prophesying a dazzling future for it.

Despite these moves towards reshaping the freight business, that side of the work continued to move into difficulties throughout the 1960s. The deficit on railway working in 1960 was £67.7 million; in 1968 it was £90.6 million, and this result was largely due to the fall in freight traffic, from 18.6 billion ton-miles in 1960 to 14.7 billion in 1968, despite the enterprise shown in stimulating train-load traffic. The reason the deficit was not far greater is that the BR staff fell from 520,000 at the beginning of 1960 to 296,000 at the end of 1968. This was due to two main causes; the 'Beeching closures' of lines and stations, and the Shirley-inspired reductions in rolling stock; moreover improved productivity stemmed from prolonged negotiations between the BRB and the railway unions, which continued into the 1970s. These had started with the single-manning agreement for diesel and electric locomotives in 1957. Savings had also been obtained from work study and incentive bonus schemes. But the greatest single factor in bringing down labour costs was undoubtedly, for most of the decade, the reduction in the number of stations (passenger and freight) between January 1960 and December 1968, from 7,450 to 3,235, marshalling yards from 878 to 184, freight wagons from 945,000 to 437,000, and coaching vehicles from 40,500 to 19,500.

A final note on the 1960s must be on the new corporate identity for BR that emerged in stages. Sir Brian Robertson had felt that Regions should have some latitude in the matter of coaching stock liveries; the main effect had been that, in theory, named trains on the Western Region would be chocolate and cream, and the Southern would retain its own green livery on the same basis. But otherwise LMS red, or a version of it, was standard. In practice, the impossibility of keeping the chocolate-and-cream vehicles to fixed rosters led to a frequent piebald appearance of trains and this rather tentative move to Regional colours fizzled out. But Sir Brian Robertson had set up a Design Panel for the BTC in 1956 'to advise on the best means of obtaining a high standard of appearance and amenity in the design of its equipment'.

The Panel really got into its stride with a number of studies — for the Glasgow suburban 'Blue Trains', for railway staff uniforms, for station signs, for ships, and for the London Midland electric rolling stock and locomotives — which culminated in 1965. In that year an exhibition was held at the Design Centre in London bringing together the main aspects of the proposed new corporate identity programme, which were illustrated in a Design Manual.

The abbreviated form 'British Rail' was standardised for all ordinary and commercial purposes, and the double-arrow symbol or totem was also launched. The long arguments over rolling stock liveries were settled, it was hoped permanently, by standardising on blue lower panels and grey upper panels for main line stock, blue (unlined) for suburban stock. Standard black-on-white signs (replacing the enamelled signs in Regional colours) for stations were also introduced progressively.

It took some time for the new, smarter uniforms to be accepted by the more conservative type of railwayman (some supervisory grades complained that they were being disguised as Norwegian skiing instructors!) but in time the early criticisms died away and the new uniforms began to be generally issued in 1966.

So BR ended the decade with a distinctive and very different character to that with which it had entered the 1960s. This was due not merely to internal developments such as have been described, but to major shifts in Government policy for the railways in the second half of the decade.

Above: One of the most reliable of the first BR Modernisation Plan diesels was the English Electric 2000hp Type 4 put straight into mid-1950s front line express service on main lines from Liverpool Street, King's Cross and Euston. No D224 heads a Euston–Liverpool express approaching Willesden in 1964. (*G.M. Kichenside*). *Below:* One of the less prolific BR diesel classes, the BTH 800hp Type 1, eventually decreed non-standard and in consequence short-lived. One of the class is seen with a cross-London freight at Gospel Oak in the late 1950s. (*British Rail*)

Above: An early dmu service with a unit in dark green livery at Hardingham station on the former GE Norwich–King's Lynn line in 1956. (*British Rail*). *Below:* A spectacular if only partially successful instalment of modernisation: the Birmingham Pullman passes West Ruislip in 1962. (*C.R.L. Coles*)

Chapter 16
Into the Seventies

For several years British Rail seemed to have reached calmer waters after the stormy passages of the later 1950s and the mid-1960s. The affable, shrewd Sir Henry Johnson piloted the vessel through this period and retired in September 1971, having seen the railways into the new decade where new problems awaited it.

What sort of a railway had emerged from the 1960s? It was considerably scaled-down in size but not all the cutbacks envisaged under reshaping had materialised. The former Midland Railway Anglo-Scottish route via Settle and Carlisle remained open — mainly for freight — largely because higher speeds on the West Coast Main Line might make it essential to have a secondary route for slower traffic. The East Coast route remained a principal artery, the idea of concentrating London-Edinburgh traffic on Euston having been shelved. A campaign had been launched by BR which in February 1970 persuaded the Government to authorise extension of the London Midland electrification — the so-called 'Weaver to Wearer' project, carrying the wires north to Glasgow from Weaver Junction near Crewe. The 1967 electrification of all services between London, Birmingham, Liverpool and Manchester had produced an upsurge in traffic and receipts, which illustrated the 'sparks effect' at its most dramatic. Lurking in the wings remained the Advanced Passenger Train; but a significant possible rival was first mentioned in the Annual Report for 1969, in these words: 'particular attention was paid to a light-weight version of the Bo-Bo locomotive — a type of traction unit which could be used in a multiple-unit formation for Inter-City services'. In the next year, the concept of HST had emerged. 'Design and development continued on a high-speed diesel passenger train capable of operation at speeds up to 125mph, and work had begun on the first prototype.'. A model of the vulgarly-named 'flying banana' was shown as an exhibit in the BR contribution to European Conservation Year. Development and testing continued until, at the end of BR's first 25 years, the first 125mph trains were nearly ready to enter service.

A good many people saw the HST as the engineers' reply to the scientists who had been working for so long on the APT — a demonstration that it may be preferable to capitalise on what is readily available, rather than keep on chasing perfection. A touch of inter-departmental rivalry was hinted at. But BR's planners were at pains to insist that the two were complementary to each other rather than alternatives.

The fact was, that a kind of 'sound barrier' exists on railways at speeds of around 125mph. Up to that speed, conventional signalling (with adaptations) and only slightly modified operating practice is involved. Raising speeds to 150mph or over involves, to a considerable extent, re-thinking the railway. This had not been fully appreciated when the APT was first envisaged. The Japanese had appreciated it, with their Shinkansen trains inaugurated in 1964. At that date these had certainly represented the most advanced rail technology in the world, but were kept just inside the 'sound barrier', since 130mph was the ceiling.

The French had carried out a series of spectacular tests with electric locomotives as early as 1954/55 under special conditions, which had established that speeds of over 200mph were technically possible (despite the occasional melting of the pantograph contact strips!) but the first 125mph regular daily services in France did not start until 1967 with the 'Capitole' express followed by the 'Aquitaine' in 1971, both locomotive-hauled formations.

The next great leap forward was however to involve the building of an entirely new railway — Paris-Sud-Est — aligned for very high speed in all respects, before the target of 300km/hr (187mph) for sustained running, could be achieved.

Even then, on second thoughts, the target speed was brought down from 300km/hr to 255km/hr (160mph).

With the evidence that had been accumulating of the commercial success of high speed by rail — in Japan and France as well as Britain — and in view of the virtual certainty that BR would not receive Government financial support for new high speed railways (as the abandonment of the Channel Tunnel direct line was to demonstrate later), it was inevitable that Britain should pin its hopes on obtaining high speed over existing routes by the APT.

But in 1972 this project was still eluding quick realisation, and the HST seemed to be the answer to prayer. Meanwhile, at last the standard of main line passenger comfort was being rapidly improved as the Mark IId and IIe series coaches came into service on the prime routes. While not perhaps offering quite such a high standard as the 'Grand Confort' coaches of the SNCF's 'Aquitaine', they were a vast improvement on anything that had gone before. Only the necessity of including Mark I catering vehicles, often giving a rough ride, marred the new standard of express train comfort, which was coupled with 100mph running on the most important services by both LMR electric locomotives and East Coast route 'Deltics'. Elsewhere 90mph was achieved wherever the maximum line speed prescribed by the Civil Engineer permitted.

The railway of the early 1970s had also become one in which continuous welded rail was becoming standard on main routes. Associated with concrete sleepers, 'Pandrol' fastenings and a greater depth of ballast, it offered a track that could withstand the stresses of very high speed trains and yet require less maintenance than jointed track, accepting the new methods of mechanised tracklaying and maintenance.

The first really modern railway station resembling a good airport terminal now existed in the new Euston. The glamour of the new electrified railway had not yet worn off, nor had riding begun to deteriorate. The branch and secondary passenger services were supported by specific grants from the Ministry, although BR was told sternly that the freight

141

business must be self-supporting. Superficially, therefore, the system which Sir Henry Johnson handed over to his successor as Chairman, the Rt Hon Richard Marsh, the ex-Minister of Transport who had succeeded Barbara Castle, looked to be in fairly good shape.

Looking more closely, however, there were causes for concern. Costs were rising all the time at an alarming rate, and though BR no longer was hampered by statutory restrictions upon charging to any significant extent, the Government's policy for controlling inflation had let to the use of the Prices and Incomes Board powers to refuse consent for general increases sought by BR in 1967, and a new policy of 'market pricing' — charging not simply by mileage but according to estimates of 'what the traffic will bear' (in the classic railway phrase) — was embarked upon.

A fundamental change had taken place in the relationship between the freight and the passenger businesses, as these figures show.

	Percentage of total traffic receipts	
	1948	1972
Passenger fares and charges	35.8	46.1
Government passenger grants	—	11.5
Parcels, mail, etc.	8.8	11.6
Freight rates and charges	55.4	30.8
	100.0	100.0

The railways had traditionally derived more than half their receipts from freight carried by 'goods train'; now the proportion was less than one-third. British Rail had become predominantly a passenger line. Traditionally, too, it had been assumed that the freight business was the more profitable; now it was clearly being carried on the back of the passenger traffic.

It was no wonder that the Board was looking for revenue from its other activities. In 1972 the ships contributed £3.3 millions net, the hotels (with rail catering) £1.4 million, and sales of property £13.9 millions. BR was and is one of the nation's six largest landowners, with a net rental income about the same as that of the Crown Estates and Church Commissioners combined. Ever since nationalisation there had been both external and internal pressures to make better use of land not required for railway operational purposes and to exploit development potential. The external pressure often came from local authorities who felt they should have first claim on land in the ownership of a public corporation.

The BTC had been pressed to do something about surplus railway land. In the 1950s, it appointed a Committee (of which I was Secretary) to look at the surplus land owned by *all* the Executives in the Euston/King's Cross/St Pancras area. Marked on a map of the district, the total 'dead land' looked vast, including canalside areas and the derelict site of Somers Town goods station. We proposed to hover over the territory in a helicopter but decided against such inflation of our expenses! Little came of our survey, as everyone had good reasons why we must wait for new ideas which were just around the corner. It was another example of the BTC's inability to push the Executives in any direction in which they did not want to go.

However, once the development boom of the sixties was well under way the BRB was firmly in the saddle, and it decided to take property development out of the hands of the Regions and centralise it, with the intention of imparting more drive in the exploitation of development potential. The Government required the railway surplus land to be offered in the first instance to local authorities, which sometimes led to delay and frustration owing to inability of a local authority to obtain Government loan sanction. A lot of delay and abortive work was involved.

Meanwhile the BRB had become entirely sold on the idea of exploiting the full commercial potential of major sites and had decided that the best way to achieve this would be in partnership with established developers. Unfortunately the Board was rather late in entering this speculative and tricky area, and sometimes insisted upon terms that the developers considered insufficiently attractive to them. However, a number of major schemes, particularly for major station reconstruction combined with office or shopping centre development, were brought to a successful conclusion, including Birmingham (New Street). A major disappointment was the refusal of planning permission to utilise the vast air space over the new Euston Station. This seemed all the more illogical in view of the grant of permission for a huge tower block in the Euston Road a few hundred yards away. (Only years later was a modified development at Euston permitted.) Sir Henry Johnson took a great personal interest in this aspect of the Board's work and after his retirement himself became Chairman of a leading property company.

His successor, Richard Marsh, proved to be an effective spokesman for the railways on radio and television. Although he took over in a period when BR's finances had been temporarily stabilised, he could see that the relentless increase in costs was certain to recreate financial problems. He energetically espoused the APT, and promoted the export of British Rail technology, backed by the Derby Technical Centre, through the formation in 1970 of a BR subsidiary consultancy company, Transportation Systems and Market Research Ltd, commonly known as Transmark. He also immediately discerned the advantages to BR if the Channel Tunnel was built and, unlike all his predecessors except Sir Brian Robertson, gave it enthusiastic personal support. (Curiously for an ex-Labour Cabinet Minister, he enjoyed more support from the Conservative Government in the first year or two after he took over, than subsequently from the Labour Government that took office in 1974.)

In 1970 an extraordinary incident took place. A boy trespasser accidentally set fire to Robert Stephenson's historic Britannia Bridge over the Menai Strait, a vital link in the principal rail and sea service to Ireland. The cost of reconstruction was very heavy, as were the incidental losses to the shipping and rail services. It took 32 months before trains could again link Anglesey with the mainland and connect with the railway ships at Holyhead. The bridge was extensively rebuilt, with new steel arches supporting Stephenson's famous tubular structure.

In 1971 it was announced that a modern computerised system for controlling and monitoring freight traffic was in sight. Entitled TOPS, Total Operations Processing System, it involved putting on a computer all relevant data regarding freight movement including locomotive and wagon availability and movements, enabling current location to be instantly established and arrival at destination to be accurately forecast in a way that had been impossible previously. TOPS was modelled on a system developed on the Southern Pacific Railroad of the USA where it had proved an operational, commercial and financial boon. The authority given in 1971 was not to bear fruit for between three and four years. A somewhat wry comment can be made that if TOPS had been in operation 20 years previously, it might have so significantly improved the quality of service — and reduced the cost of providing it — that the wagon-load traffic would not have melted away as it did in the 1960s.

In BR's 25th year, the Annual Report for the first time departed from the standard, very sober format of HM Stationery Office and appeared as a 'glossy', with many colour illustrations interspersed in the text. It was essentially a Marsh production, lively, and punching home its main points. The most striking feature however was comparison of the still much-criticised BR of 1972 with the railways of the last year before nationalisation, in a telling pictogram illustrating the key figures, which showed 1972 as a percentage of 1947, as follows:

Passenger-miles	77 per cent
Net Ton-miles	62 per cent

So business was down overall, between two-thirds and three-quarters of 1947, but — and this the illustration showed most effectively — productivity was greater, very obviously, since:

Staff	only 31 per cent
Carriages	" 44 " "
Wagons	" 22 " "

So Marsh pleaded for more investment, asking 'that the nation will never again allow itself to be guilty of lack of foresight in planning for transport needs'. After 25 years of nationalisation, he was entitled to ask this; he was over-optimistic if he really expected it to happen.

To celebrate the 150 years of railway development since the opening in 1825 of the Stockton & Darlington Railway, the BRB issued a volume entitled *Rail 150*. The final section (there were four contributors), written by Ian Waller, contained these words. 'As British Rail celebrate their anniversary they can look to the future with greater optimism than for many years past. The long years of decline have been halted and both in Britain and abroad there is a new awareness of the role that railways can and must provide in modern industrialised societies. Far from being a nineteenth-century anachronism in the age of cars and planes they have the potential to solve many of the transport problems that the internal combustion engine has created, and to do so often more cheaply and efficiently.' One would like to think that this message would finally get home to BR's political masters.

Chapter 17
The Railwaymen

Any idealist who imagined that nationalisation would usher in a Golden Age of industrial relations on the railways would have been disappointed. In fact, industrial relations have been more difficult, and instances of industrial action of one kind or another more frequent, than in company days. This has not been a consequence of nationalisation but of radical changes in the climate in which industrial relations on the railways have had to be conducted. In the years after the war it had to be accepted, if slowly, that there must be a contraction in the total volume of railway business due to competition from public and private road transport, and to the reduction in transport of coal and other heavy goods which had been the mainstay of the companies' finances. This was certainly not accepted by the unions until the later 1950s, and even then, with optimistic pronouncements by management about the effects of the Modernisation Plan, the impact was temporarily deadened.

But at the same time, because of the rise in the general standard of living, the old simple yard-stick of the cost-of-living index in determining changes in wage levels became outmoded. Comparability with pay in other industries took its place, and the increasingly difficult financial position of the railways affected their ability to meet wage claims based on comparability with the high wages which expanding or more prosperous industries were tending to offer. And the criterion of comparability was in itself a cause of wage inflation. No sooner had parity been secured in one industry than others were provided with a new starting point for further claims, and this leap-frogging gave the spiral of increases an upward push.

There was another deep-rooted change in the position of railwaymen vis-a-vis workers in more prosperous industries. Before the war, the security of railway employment was greatly valued. There was little difficulty in securing suitable staff, if the minimum railway wage over the country as a whole kept in touch with the basic agricultural wage and there were adequate differentials for skill and responsibility. But by 1948 recruitment of suitable staff had often become difficult, particularly in London and the chief industrial centres. The dwindling nucleus of older railwaymen found it hard to retain the element of pride in the job which characterised many of them before the war.

The unions (officially) and groups of railwaymen (unofficially) from time to time were induced to take industrial action in the form of strikes or 'working to rule'. Some strikes were extremely damaging, as, for example, that by the Associated Society of Locomotive Engineers and Firemen in 1955, which lasted 17 days and was estimated to have lost the BTC some £12 million. Since some drivers, particularly in North-East England and on the LMR, belonged to the NUR and consequently remained at work, this led to ill feeling between the unions which persisted for a long time afterwards. But an unexpected consequence appeared; the strike demonstrated that is was no longer the case that a complete railway stoppage must paralyse the nation. Coal, iron and steel and electricity supply were seriously affected, as were London commuters on their way to work; but elsewhere the vast expansion in road transport enabled the economic life of the country to struggle on. Some of the traffic diverted during the stoppage never returned to rail, so that in the long run employment on the railways was seriously affected.

The fundamental issue between management and the unions was that the latter felt that their members were entitled to share properly in the general improvement in real wages which was taking place, quite irrespective of the railways' ability to meet the cost. In their view the financial position of the railways should not be the determinant, since behind a

Bold Sir Brian Robertson

(With apologies to Mr. A. A. Milne)

SIR BRIAN had a railway which *sometimes* had some trains on,
  A brightly coloured railway—it was always in the red.
Yet, on any Easter Sunday or (more recently) Whit Monday,
  He went among his railwaymen, and this is what he said:
            I am Sir Brian (*Chuff Chuff!*)
            I am Sir Brian (*Chu! Chu!*)
            I am Sir Brian,
            As bold as a lion,
            Pray, what can I do to please you?

In spite of his munificence, Sir Brian woke one morning
  To find his trains weren't running, since the drivers were not there.
To maintain their differential, they wished treatment preferential,
  So he called on Mr. Baty and addressed him from a chair:
            I am Sir Brian (*All aboard!*)
            I am Sir Brian (*Right away!*)
            I am Sir Brian,
            As bold as a lion,
            I'll give nothing—until I give way.

Sir Brian needed money, which he'd promised to the railwaymen,
  On behalf of all the owners (by Act of Parliament).
Although they'd had no say in it, they'd have to put their pay in it,
  So—A NOTICE TO THE PASSENGERS—and this is how it went:
            I am Sir Brian (*Peep! Peep!*)
            I am Sir Brian (*Puff! Puff!*)
            I am Sir Brian,
            As bold as a lion,
            You passengers don't pay enough.

The passengers arose from the cold, damp waiting-rooms.
  They did not get their tickets, since they all were seeing red.
They nobbled the inspectors, and insulted the collectors,
  Until they reached Sir Brian, and this is what they said:
            You are Sir Brian? (*Oh! No!*)
            You are Sir Brian? *It's true!*)
            You are Sir Brian,
            As bold as a lion,
            Well, sir, this is *your* Waterloo!

                              HENRY FAIRLIE

nationalised industry stood the financial resources of the whole nation.

It became evident soon after nationalisation that the issue — and the consequent unrest — could not be solved within the railways' own machinery of negotiation. The Government intervened by setting up a series of Courts or Committees of Inquiry. Two of these were significant.

It was during such an Inquiry in 1955 that Lord Cameron made his famous statement that 'having willed the end, the Nation must will the means .... in broad terms, the railwayman should be no worse case than his colleague in a comparable industry.' But what was a comparable industry? What was comparability? How could the jobs be compared?

In 1958 a Committee known as the Guillebaud Committee (after its Chairman, a distinguished economist) collected over 1,500 reports on railway work and 600 on work in other industries. The Committee then listed the deviation from railway rates of pay in the 137 cases in which job comparability was felt to be established and found that the deviation varied very largely, both above and below. It also compared the rates of pay of the lowest graded railway staff with those of 18 basic grades in outside industry. In this case there was a less spread-out deviation, averaging about 10% over the railway figures. The Committee concluded that this could be assumed to be the extent to which the level of railway wages fell below those in the country as a whole. The estimated cost of implementing the Guillebaud recommendation was £33 million, a sum which brought into question, in Parliament and elsewhere, the whole future of the railways.

It was evident that in a labour-intensive industry like the railways, with such acute financial problems, labour costs must be reduced through greater productivity if the industry were to survive. Strong efforts were made to have specific undertakings of increased productivity included in the continuing series of pay settlements.

An exact measure of productivity in a complex structure such as the railways is impossible to determine but some indication of what was achieved is given by the fact that between 1960 and 1968 staff numbers fell from 518,000 to 307,000, a reduction of 41%, while during the same period production (based on the crude but only available yardsticks of passenger-miles, ton-miles and train-miles) fell by only 20%.

Much of this massive reduction in staff came from modernisation, for example by replacing steam locomotives by a much smaller number of diesel and electric locomotives and multiple-unit trains: by the mechanisation of permanent way maintenance; and by the introduction of power signalling. There were measures of rationalisation such as concentration of coal depots, the development of block trains for oil, cement, etc, and the adoption of method study techniques in the layout of depots and stations.

Secondly, there was the closing of uneconomic or unnecessary lines, culminating in the Beeching Plan and thirdly, there was the introduction of work study incentive schemes, which by 1970, covered some 100,000 staff.

The process of contracting staff numbers involved an almost continuous process of consultation and dissemination of information, of seeking means to help men to find other jobs or in moving their homes, and in helping them to re-train in alternative skills. And a tribute is certainly due to the railwaymen for the way in which they adapted themselves to such changes without serious unrest. It was perhaps fortunate that this problem could be settled at a time when opportunities of alternative employment in outside industry were greater, particularly in industrial areas, than was later the case.

Another important factor was the introduction of redundancy payments, first made when the Midland & Great Northern line in East Anglia was closed and nearly 1000 men became redundant, many of whom were located in areas where it was difficult to find alternative jobs. A greater problem arose later when 13 of the 29 railway workshops were closed and the labour force in the workshops was reduced from 62,000 to 42,000. A more refined scheme was devised which provided a lump sum payment, dependent on length of service plus continuing payments for a maximum period while the man remained unemployed.

While much of the process of increasing productivity was thus carried through with comparative smoothness, special issues arose which raised particular difficulties. First was the obvious suggestion that diesel and electric locomotives should be single-manned since there was no task comparable to that of the fireman on a steam locomotive. Equally, the operation of fully-fitted freight trains eliminated the traditional function of the goods guard, that of actng as brakesman. For seven years, from 1960 to 1967, unions and management argued over these questions, with incentive schemes to increase productivity being put forward by the Board. The Government eventually intervened to set up a Court of Inquiry under A.J. (later Sir Jack) Scamp, which led to a Manning Agreement (a compromise measure, as was to be expected) being signed in October 1965.

In 1966 intensive thought was being given to incentive schemes for all trainmen. Bonus freight train working had in fact existed in the North Eastern Region for many years (inherited from the LNER) but new methods of operation called for a new approach. Freight train operation by diesel traction, with power braking of all wagons, needed new rules compared with those applicable to steam locomotives and loose-coupled wagons. There was prolonged argument over this question and Mr Scamp was again called in as a referee. The most acute problems were the surplus of footplate staff arising from the change of motive power, the similar reduction in the need for goods guards, and the Board's desire to link pay with productivity.

At the beginning of 1967 L.F. (later Sir Leonard) Neal was appointed to the Board as its industrial relations Member. He had been a trade union organiser and then had entered management in which capacity he had negotiated the famous Fawley productivity agreement, often considered a model of its kind. He took a prominent part in the difficult negotiations which followed in the next few years until he left the Board in October 1971.

During 1967 industrial relations became difficult in the extreme. LIFT (London International Freight Terminal) at Stratford was due to open on 19 June but was blacked by the NUR. This terminal was road and rail connected for handling international traffic by train ferry wagons or containers, with warehousing and transit sheds for BR and freight forwarding firms, with an associated Freightliner terminal. The union insisted that all traffic at the depot must be handled by railway staff, whereas the forwarding agents intended to use their own staff for their own traffic. The strike lasted a fortnight, being ended by BRB giving assurances about the future employment of the men concerned.

Another dispute with the NUR flared up in the autumn of 1967 over guards undertaking 'second man' duties on diesel and electric locomotives; and when this was settled ASLEF instituted a work-to-rule with blacking of some trains, on the ground that the agreement with the NUR breached the 1965 Manning Agreement.

Matters came to a head in 1968 when the unions demanded a general rise unconnected with productivity, and the Board put forward a 'productivity bargain' for all grades of staff except trainmen. This dispute went to the Railway Staff National Tribunal, the final stage in the statutory machinery of negotiation, which compromised by awarding an interim increase for lower paid workers, to be absorbed later into pay increases based on productivity. The unions rejected this and a work-to-rule was instituted, with a ban on overtime and rest-day working.

This led to the so-called 'Penzance Agreement'. The NUR had started its annual conference in that town on 1 July. A team from BRB, headed by L.F. Neal, descended upon them, brought in ASLEF, and succeeded in reaching agreement after many hours of intensive discussion.

This initial success led to the Board proposing and the unions accepting a conference at New Lodge, Windsor (at that

time a BR training college with residential accommodation)
where representatives of the Board and the two unions lived
and worked together for 2½ weeks until a final productivity
agreement was hammered out.

This incorporated a new grading system, creating posts of
'Railman', 'Leading railman', 'Senior railman' and 'Chargeman'
replacing former grades such as porter, just as 'secondman'
had replaced 'fireman' in the locomotive field. A new grade of
'conductor guard' was also instituted for Inter-City and other
important passenger trains, and also in cases where the duties
of guard and travelling ticket collector could be combined.

Despite the progress achieved by the Penzance and Windsor
agreements, the linking of pay with productivity still was far
from complete. And the accelerating pressure of inflation led
to workers in other industries receiving substantial increases
with no productivity strings attached; this inevitably led to
demands for similar treatment on the part of the railway
unions. Meanwhile the BRB proposed a Pay and Efficiency
Stage IV Agreement in August 1970 on which progress was
slow and general percentage increases meanwhile had to be
conceded. It was difficult to maintain the impetus towards
better industrial relations provided by the Windsor agreement.
In April 1971 the ASLEF instituted a 'work-to-rule' to bring
pressure for settlement of a pay claim; and in 1972 the Board
experienced what they described as 'exceptional pressure' on
pay levels. That year's round of pay negotiations lasted
without interruption from early March until 13 June, and
ended in a general increase of 13½ per cent in paybill costs.
Accordingly the first quarter-century of the nationalised
railways ended with industrial relations far from being
permanently eased.

The hope of closer co-operation between management and
staff in improving efficiency, which the unions had stressed
when celebrating the advent of nationalisation, looked as
though it might be realised when, only 11 months after
nationalisation, there had been established the British Transport Joint Consultative Council, intended to provide 'for the

Above: Still very 'LMS' in character, the down Caledonian passes Tring summit in 1959. (*C.R.L. Coles*). *Below:* An historic combination: Class A4 No 60022 *Mallard* passes York with the down Flying Scotsman in 1960 when the Deltics were in the offing. (*I.S. Carr*)

Above: Overdue for improvement: the 'African Village' disfiguring the elegant facade of King's Cross in the 1960s. (*British Rail*). *Below:* In contrast, Euston was totally demolished in stages during the 1960s, Hardwick's Great Hall included, to be replaced by a reasonably elegant glass and concrete structure which the planners decided could not be combined with commercial development. The trains still had to run as seen here in 1963. (*G.M. Kichenside*)

exchange of information and views upon matters of common interest .... not however being questions of wages or conditions of service'. Consultation on railway questions was also to take place at lower levels corresponding to those in the established machinery of negotiation — Local Departmental Committees, Sectional Councils, Shop, Works and Line Committees. Although the machinery looked impressive on paper, the unions often criticised it on the grounds that, after the management had decided upon changes, joint consultation was invoked at a late stage merely as a convenient channel for telling the staff what was going to happen. Consultation, it was argued, must be a two-way process. On its side, management complained that the unions often treated joint consultation as inseparable from negotiation; that they looked at management proposals solely as a means of extracting better pay or conditions, not on their merits as affecting the future prospects of the industry. An added problem was the need to observe confidentiality about policy proposals where premature disclosure might lead to ill-informed criticism or blocking moves. Management was usually able to observe confidentiality; but on the union side, this was extremely difficult and leaks led to embarrassment and complaints.

The BTC had also made an early declaration of its intention to improve staff welfare facilities and created a Joint Advisory Council for Welfare in 1948. There were still serious problems in providing amenities for railway staff comparable with those common in a well-equipped modern factory. The wide dispersal and mobility of so much of the labour force created great difficulty. Mess-rooms and similar facilities had often been rather rudimentary in company days, with old carriage bodies and lineside bothies (for permanent way workers) widely in use. During the war, canteens had been installed at many places, in conformity with Government policy for supplementing rationed food for workers in industry. But investment restrictions after the war, and later the impending disappearance of steam traction, made it impracticable to improve staff facilities at many stations and motive power depots where conditions were unsatisfactory. Station, yard and depot reconstruction and the construction of new diesel and electric maintenance centres and carriage sheds under the Modernisation Plan enabled some of the backlog to be overtaken. Added impetus was given by the passing of the Office, Shops and Railway Premises Act in 1963 which in effect removed the exemption railways had previously enjoyed from the provisions of the Factory Acts.

In the field of training and education, a patchwork of practices and facilities was inherited from the former companies. The LMS had its residential school of Transport at Derby and the Southern its smaller school in an elegant country house near Woking (transformed, in 1959, into the British Transport Staff College).

The Transport Act, 1947 required the BTC in organising training and education facilities, 'to act on lines settled with the approval of the Minister'. A general set of guide lines was laid down and formed the basis of a report which the Minister duly approved and which served to demonstrate the excellent intentions of the Commission even if no very dramatic changes took effect. Both the BTC and later the British Railways Board were more interested in the training of managers (see Chapter 24) than with greatly increasing the quality and quantity of training in the wages grades, where the practices of the former companies continued, with some modest developments such as the special one-week courses for railwaymen of all grades at Dillington House, the Somerset Education Committee's residential college.

But induction training courses for traffic staff, such as London Transport provided in its railway and bus training schools, were not provided except in a rather variable and sporadic way. It was not automatically linked with recruitment, and recruitment itself was carried out very much on traditional lines by local supervisors and staff clerks.

When I became Director of Training and Education in 1962 I tried to strengthen the existing practices. I was successful in getting a full-time Vocational Training Officer appointed and we concentrated initially upon the training of supervisors. I was unable however to obtain the necessary support or financial resources for a complete overhaul of recruitment methods, linked with universal induction training.

A service industry such as railways depends more on staff quality than any other single factor for the provision of an acceptable and efficient product. At times the emphasis has lain perhaps too much on staff numbers and labour costs, not enough on more sophisticated recruitment principles and much more thorough training and retraining of those who determine the success or failure of the task.

Chapter 18
Money Matters

Before nationalisation, in fact from 1939, the railways had been under Government control. The railway shareholders had been paid annual rentals for the use of the railways, the Government meeting all the operating costs and pocketing the receipts. The rentals for the four main line companies had since 1941 been fixed amounts, totalling £38.17 million, much less than the actual annual net earnings of the railways over most of the period.

When the railways were vested in the British Transport Commission, railway stocks were compulsorily exchanged for new Government-guaranteed British Transport 3% stock, the basis of exchange being Stock Exchange prices for railway stock which had broadly reflected the earning power under the Government's Control Agreement with the companies.

Thereafter there was no 'railway capital' as such. The BTC's liabilities for payment of interest and sinking fund charges on all its stocks were not distributed among the various Executives which managed the nationalised transport undertakings on behalf of the Commission. The Commission's accounts for 1948 set out 'Consolidated Working Results of the Principal Carrying Activities', in which there were separate tables including:

Passenger and Freight Services of British Railways; ·
Collection and Delivery and Other Road Services of BR;
Ships: passenger and cargo services of BR

Another table set out 'Consolidated Working Results of Other Principal Activities', including:

Docks, Harbours and Wharves;
Commercial Advertising;
Letting of sites, shops, etc, on premises and properties in use for transport purposes.

In this second group, the railways contributed under each head, but in no case exclusively.

So the accounts re-grouped the results of the management units. And they showed no apportioned charges for interest and the central expenses of the BTC itself. These had to be met from the aggregate net receipts of the 'activities'.

In 1948 the railway passenger and freight services, the largest single component in the consolidated BTC results, showed net traffic receipts of £26.3 million. (These cannot usefully be compared with income under the pre-nationalisation Government Control Agreement owing to differences in the activities covered.)

The Commission in its Annual Report commented that 'in any nation-wide transport undertaking covering the various forms of transport, different services and different methods of transport will show unequal degrees of profitability and will be unable to contribute at a uniform rate to overhead charges'. The overall result of the operations in 1948, after meeting interest and central charges, was a small deficit of net revenue for the BTC as a whole amounting to £4.7 million. This position was to continue, with various ups and downs, until the mid-1950s, when it worsened abruptly.

Railway net traffic receipts (including the working of the road collection and delivery services, but excluding the miscellaneous receipts from other activities carried on by BR) fluctuated in the early years as follows:

	£million
1948	+ 22.4
1949	+. 9.0
1950	+ 23.5
1951	+ 31.7
1952	+ 37.0
1953	+ 33.0
1954	+ 14.8
1955	+ 0.1
1956	− 16.5

These results would of course have looked different if an appropriate portion of the Commission's capital debt had been allocated to the railways, and interest and sinking fund charges had been levied against the railway receipts. Allowing for the low rate of interest (3 or 3½%) on the original issue of British Transport stock, the position would not have been too serious, except in 1949, up to 1953; but the rapid decline thereafter would have shown up more disastrously.

After 1956 the Commission did begin to allocate its central charges, including interest, over its principal activities. There were good reasons for this. In negotiations over wages, if capital charges were not allocated, it was easy for the unions to argue that they were not relevant to the issue. Again, in applications to the Transport Tribunal set up under the 1947 Act to regulate the Commission's charges, the trend of costs was the usual reason for seeking authority for increased fares and rates. The Tribunal was entitled to ask, if interest and other central charges had to be covered in part from railway receipts, just how much this share amounted to. So the Commission, when putting a freight charging scheme to the Tribunal in 1956, estimated that 70 per cent of its interest and other central charges should be allocated to the railways.

Using this proportion, and bringing together the rail passenger and freight receipts and the collection and delivery service results, Mr. W.T. Parker has calculated* that after meeting central charges, the true results for the years 1948-56 would have been:

	Surplus or Deficit £million
1948	− 8.2
1949	− 23.4
1950	− 10.8
1951	− 0.7
1952	+ 3.7
1953	− 2.4
1954	− 21.6
1955	− 38.2
1956	− 57.5

* in an unpublished study 'British Railways Financial Performance and Government Policy, 1948 to 1975'.

By 1956 the Commission as a whole was in financial trouble, mainly because of the railways' deteriorating position. The net receipts of the other activities in that year gave some assistance — British Road Services £1.8 million, bus groups £5.3 million, London Transport £4.5 million, shipping services £1.8 million, for instance — but this was not enough to keep the Commission's head above water. The Government had to come to its assistance with the Transport (Railway Finances) Act 1957 which enabled the BTC to borrow money to cover railway deficits in the years 1956 to 1962, to a maximum of £250 million. This measure was supposed, in the Commission's own words, to reflect 'the confidence of Parliament in the Commission's undertaking'; but it proved to be only a palliative. The 'confidence' was largely based upon the prediction that the Modernisation Plan of 1955 would produce a total improvement of £85 millions a year in the financial results of the railways, which was sadly over-optimistic.

In 1961 the Government published a White Paper 'The Financial and Economic Obligations of the Nationalised Industries', in which it was declared that the state corporations should 'break even', ie bring revenue in line with expenditure, averaged over a five-year period, and also build up reserves. The Government would fix investment limits for two years ahead, and would expect to be consulted before charges were altered substantially.

This expression of pious hope was unrealistic in the case of the railways, where the position was getting worse instead of better. This was a major factor in the decision, implemented in the Transport Act, 1962, to separate the railways from the other undertakings in the BTC, give them almost complete commercial freedom, and write down the capital debt attributable to them.

The net deficits on railway working (and road collection and delivery) between 1956, when the new borrowing powers were given, and the abolition of the Commission, were as follows:-

	Traffic working £million	Net overall deficit £million
1957	− 27.1	− 68.1
1958	− 48.1	− 90.1
1959	− 42.0	− 84.0
1960	− 67.7	− 112.7
1961	− 86.9	− 135.9
1962	− 103.9	− 159.0

Clearly the £250 million of new borrowing authorised in 1956 was inadequate, even if it had been really a sound method of financing the situation. The Government, seeing no immediate alternative, increased the £250 million limit to £400 million in 1959 by the Transport (Borrowing Powers) Act of that year. It was however realised that this in itself would be quickly exceeded and in 1960 BR ceased to take borrowings on this account. The Chancellor of the Exchequer provided in his Budget for grants to be made to the BTC in place of the loans taken under the 1957 Act. There was no statutory backing for this at the time and the payments were put 'above the line' in the national accounts and were a direct charge on the taxpayers' money. The position was 'legalised' by the 1962 Act.

What were the reasons for this disappointing performance? First of all, a decline in freight traffic started in 1956, and by 1962 net ton-miles were only about 80 per cent of the 1948 figures. Passenger traffic held up pretty well until 1961, declining slightly thereafter.

But costs were rising continuously. Pressure for increased wages and salaries was almost impossible to resist; on occasion, Government intervention to prevent industrial action forced the Commission's hand. Other industries faced rising costs but were able to preserve equilibrium by raising their charges proportionately. The Commission's charges were subject to the Transport Tribunal's approval, intended to be given through comprehensive charges schemes for all the BTC's transport businesses. The preparation of Schemes took a very considerable time and interim 'blanket' increases were applied for in the meantime. Delay in approving these pushed the railway financial position into difficulty. Then there was unhelpful Government intervention which had started as long ago as 1952 when the Minister of Transport issued a formal direction to the BTC not to increase charges for rail travel outside the London area although such increases had been authorised by the Transport Tribunal.

Some slight relief was given by the Transport Act, 1953, which provided that the charges embodied in schemes should only be maxima, and that the railways should be free to fix the actual charges within these limits. But Transport Tribunal approval was still needed and the machinery was slow and cumbersome. A Freight Charges Scheme was submitted in draft in 1955 but could not be brought into effect until 1957. Year after year the Commission set out the estimated losses of revenue caused by its inability to increase charges promptly in line with increases in costs.

By the 1962 Transport Act, the Government abolished the Commission and placed the railways under the new British Railways Board. Part of the total capital liabilities of the BTC were allocated to the new BRB. Out of a total BTC debt of £2,437 million (made up of £1,144 million British Transport Stock and £993 million advances from the Minister of Transport), a 'commencing capital debt to the Minister' of £1,562 million was charged to the Railways Board. However, only part of this was interest-bearing, namely £857 million; the remainder, £705 million, was free of interest and described as 'suspended debt'. In theory, the former represented 'live' assets' acquired since the Modernisation Plan; the latter 'dead assets' acquired at nationalisation, such as permanent way and structures.

The intention was that 'business management' coupled with full commercial freedom, would enable the railways to break even and pay interest on the 'live' capital debt. To promote this, the 1962 Act removed the requirement to prepare Charges Schemes and to obtain the approval of the Transport Tribunal. Apart from passenger fares in London and traffic competitive with coastal shipping, the railway now had virtually complete commercial freedom.

However, the other two factors — stagnant or declining traffic levels and increasing costs — continued to apply, despite the effects of the Beeching re-shaping and the many new developments of the 1960s. The BRB was still in deficit over the years 1963-68.

	Deficit on Railway Operating*	Total BRB deficit, after interest and net income from other activities
	£million	£million
1963	− 87.1	− 133.9
1964	− 73.3	− 120.9
1965	− 79.5	− 132.4
1966	− 78.3	− 134.7
1967	− 97.4	− 153.0
1968	− 90.6	− 147.4

In 1967 the Government decided that all future major price increases by the nationalised industries would be referred to the National Board for Prices and Incomes. The Board reported on BR charges twice in 1968 and once in 1969, and the BR proposals were scaled down, modified or delayed in ways that seriously affected receipts.

Meanwhile the worsening situation had led to the Transport Act, 1968, which drastically reconstructed BR's finances. The 'suspended debt' was extinguished altogether and the 'live' or interest-bearing debt was reduced to £365 million. There were balance sheet adjustments to reflect the value of assets transferred from the British Railways Board to the new National Freight Corporation. Other assistance was given in the form of grants to cover the cost of removing surplus track and signalling equipment.

But the most important financial provision of the 1968 Act was the specific grants to be paid by the Minister to the Board for unremunerative passenger services. These grants amounted to £61.2 millions in 1969, slowly increasing annually to reach £68.2 million in 1972.

* including road collection and delivery, but not BRB's miscellaneous activities.

The combined effect of these measures was to restore the railways to the position of being financially self-supporting, which they had not enjoyed since the mid-1950s. The grants were treated, quite legitimately, as income of the passenger business. In summary, the BRB's results in the four years after the passing of the 1968 Act were:

	Railway Operating Surplus*	BRB surplus or deficit after interest and net income from other activities
	£million	£million
1969	+ 41.0	+ 14.7
1970	+ 39.4	+ 9.5
1971	+ 17.2	− 15.4
1972	+ 7.3	− 26.2

This financial 'second honeymoon' was drawing to a close at the end of 1972! But it had removed, temporarily at any rate, the stigma of 'deficit' which many railwaymen had resented, since they were merely doing, to the best of their ability the job that the Government had instructed them to do.

Finally, the caution expressed in the first paragraph of this chapter about making general assumptions about BR's financial performance needs to be repeated even more strongly if one is trying to estimate what would have been the position of the railways had they not been nationalised. The railway companies of course had other revenues than those derived from the railway itself. To the railway traffic net receipts there was added the net receipts from shipping services, dock and harbour operations, hotels, refreshment rooms, commercial advertising, and property management. In addition there was a substantial income from investments in bus companies and a growing income from investments in road haulage concerns, travel agencies, etc. There also would have been some offsetting losses, though very much smaller in total, on the railway-owned canals and on the operation of restaurant cars.

Had the railways not been nationalised, their financial problems on the railway side would therefore have been eased

* excluding road collection and delivery operations, transferred to NFC in 1969, and also miscellaneous BRB activities.

by other activities and no doubt the companies would have sought to diversify, by investment of their substantial liquid resources in other activities. Whether this would in the long run have enabled them to survive without some form of subsidy from public funds is, to say the least, doubtful.

A problem that has already been mentioned in Chapter 11 is that of investment resources. In the early years after national-isation, the period of continuing post-war austerity, successive Governments imposed sharp restrictions on investment which included not merely capital expenditure but replacement of worn-out or obsolete assets, the cost of which was met from renewal funds built up from revenue — in other words, by internal financing. The restrictions were applied, first by physical controls — steel supplies and building labour permits, for instance — and later by expenditure limits. The story of the Modernisation Plan is that of a successful campaign to persuade the Government to relax these controls for a time and to provide new money for railway investment.

But the very success of the Plan in this respect led to the uncovering of several awkward facts. The section of the Plan entitled 'economics' admitted that 'it is obviously difficult to forecast in detail the economic effects of the Plan'. Of the total outlay of roughly £1,200 millions, it was estimated that some £400 million would be provided from internal sources. Interest on the balance of new capital required, the additional depreciation charges and what was described as 'the rectification of the inadequacy of current net traffic receipts' would amount to some £80 million a year. Against this, the BTC 'were of the opinion that the actual return from the investment should be of the order of £85 million a year, and might conceivably be much greater.' The build-up of the £85 million was:-

	£ million
Improvement in working results (lower costs and more revenue) from passenger services	35
Improvement in working results of freight services	60
	95
Less increased expenses on common items (track, etc.)	10
	85

It was accepted that individual financial justification had to be obtained, so far as possible, for each major instalment of investment following approval of the Plan in principle. This was where difficulties arose, because much of the outlay could only contribute in a general way to the improvement of efficiency, and specific financial benefits could not be attributed to it. Raising the standard of track was an example. On the other hand, new concentration schemes for marshalling yards, for instance, would generally throw up direct economies from the closure of numerous small yards and the reduction in trip train working between them. Replacement of steam locomotives by diesel locomotives at higher costs generally had to be justified on estimated higher utilisation and performance expectations.

By comparison, in company days when technical standards were more static, the problems of justifying investment had been simpler. Use of renewal funds to maintain the assets in proper condition was not questioned. On the other hand, capital expenditure upon, for instance, electrification schemes had to be rigorously tested to ensure that it would earn sufficient net revenue to cover more than the market rate of interest.

Now, moving to a much less settled state of affairs, with new and expensive technological developments, despite a difficult commercial situation, posed problems, aggravated by the need to convince sceptical civil servants in the Ministry of Transport as well as the even more critical Treasury that stood behind them. All the nationalised industries have experienced the differences in outlook between those basically trained to control and limit public expenditure, and those who understand that investment is the life-blood of a business.

The controversy over the financial justification for the London Midland electrification led to the establishment of more sophisticated procedures, laid down in new 'Works and Equipment Regulations' which had to be followed in submitting all proposals for expenditure of a non-recurrent character — whether capital or otherwise. Eventually discounted cash flow techniques became mandatory, with test discount rates laid down by the Treasury, in accordance with policy set out in White Papers attempting to give standard financial objectives to all the nationalised industries — a pretty hopeless task in view of the wide difference in their needs and circumstances.

Lastly, for projects which were desirable on social or general grounds, but which lacked specific financial justification by conventional appraisal methods, social cost-benefit analysis, first applied to the M1 Motorway project and the London Transport Victoria Line, began to be called in, where BR felt it could establish a case.

Even so, the BRB felt constrained to complain in almost every Annual Report about the inadequacy of the investment ceilings imposed by the Government, and the disrupting effect upon all planning of the short-term variations and lack of security which resulted from Treasury cash control. There was also more than a suspicion that the Ministry of Transport was inclined to fight harder for funds to carry out its own highway development policies than for money for British Rail. In the BRB Annual Report for 1972, Richard Marsh wrote 'In terms of capital investment for renewal, research, development and improvement the railways' share has not been comparable with the millions poured into other forms of transport. New motorways and trunk roads, with all that they mean in environmental offence, between them represent a national investment every year more than five times greater than investment in British Rail, and even then most of the railway investment is to keep the system going'.

With the exception of the 'honeymoon' period of the Modernisation Plan, this has been a perennial theme throughout BR's first quarter-century.

Chapter 19

The Shipping Story

Unlike the railway itself, the shipping business of British Rail has been a story of very nearly continuous growth. Considering the acute problems that many deep-sea shipping companies have faced, with the virtual disappearance of the passenger liner as it used to exist, the success of the short-sea services has been remarkable. The chief factors have been the phenomenal, almost uninterrupted growth in travel to and from the Continent, accompanied by a huge rise in motoring holidays. These have meant that, even though airlines have taken most of the business travel, and have dominated the 'inclusive tour' holiday market, there has still been a substantial, if rather static, traffic in 'classic' passengers, using train and ship. Over and above this has been a rapidly expanding passenger car-ferry business, and on the freight side a substantial growth in container traffic and an even more spectacular increase in roll-on, roll-off road lorry crossings. The significance of the latter is shown by the fact that, while in 1956 there were little more than 500 lorry crossings by ferry, in 1963 there were nearly 17,000 and in 1972, over 80,000 lorries or trailers were carried.

But at nationalisation little of this spectacular development could be forecast. Each of the four main line companies contributed ships to the nationalised railway, 122 in total, aggregating 60,000 net registered tons. Oil-fired steam turbine ships were then still the standard for the principal services; 92 had been chartered by the Government at various stages of the war and a number had been lost.

The transfer from company management to that of the Railway Executive was initially made by leaving the ships in Regional hands, but putting the headquarters co-ordinating and policy functions in the hands of a Chief Officer (Marine) and a Chief Officer (Continental). The Executive soon produced a five-year shipbuilding programme designed to bring back the fleet to pre-war strength; traffic was already buoyant and capacity during the summer peak was heavily taxed. Container traffic was beginning to build up, especially to Ireland, both the Republic and Ulster.

New ships, some ordered by the companies before nationalisation, were also coming into service, notably the SS *Amsterdam* for the Harwich-Hook of Holland Route, the SS *Brighton* for the Newhaven-Dieppe route, the SS *Normannia* for Southampton-Havre, and the SS *Lord Warden*, the largest car carrier yet built, for the Dover-Boulogne route.

Disaster hit the shipping services in 1953. In January the MV *Princess Victoria*, a stern-loading car-carrier on the Stranraer-Larne route encountered very heavy seas, described as 'approaching the limits of experience'; a huge wave smashed over the stern of the vessel, burst the car doors and caused the ship to founder with the loss of 133 lives. The principal cause was that the freeing ports were unable to cope with this vast weight of water. This was an almost unique incident in the very high safety record of railway steamers. Yet luck was against the service that year; in May the SS *Duke of York*, which had been drafted from the Irish services to the Hook of Holland route, was in collision with an American vessel, involving some loss of life, while 35 miles out from Harwich.

After the British Transport Commission replaced the Railway Executive, the Commission left the shipping services mainly in the hands of the Regions under their Area Boards, but created at headquarters a Shipping Sub-Commission. The Commission, or certain members of it, were inclined to the view that the railway companies had dispersed their activities too widely and that it was wrong in principle that railwaymen should be running businesses such as shipping and hotels, for instance. This had been one of the reasons for the 'compartmenting' of the BTC's activities between Executives, referred to in Chapter 3. But hitherto shipping had not been detached

Above: Main line electrification at last: 25kV electric locomotive on an express passenger train at Runcorn station, London Midland Region, in 1962. (*British Rail*). *Below:* The dawn of Mark II rolling stock: prototype XP64 hauled by a 2750hp Brush diesel locomotive in 1964. (*British Rail*)

Above: Redundant! Modernised motive power depot coaling stages at Crewe North which lasted little more than a decade. (*L&GRP/David & Charles*). *Below:* Steam in decline: Clan class 4–6–2 No 72007 on an up train at Carlisle, and leaking badly, in 1965. (*I. S. Carr*)

from railway management, nor indeed had the railway-owned 'packet ports' — Folkestone, Newhaven, Fishguard, Harwich (Parkeston Quay) and so on. The Commission had accepted the argument that the railway steamers were merely in effect prolongations of railway routes. Another reason was perhaps because the shipping services had been expanding and were profitable. The only real misgivings the Commission had felt had been from time to time over the increasing cost of new ships and also over the maintenance of the traditional links between the railways and individual ship-builders. Southern Railway ships had tended to be built by Dennys, LNER vessels by John Brown. The Commission were restive over these practices and wanted wider tendering and ordering in future.

The shipping side had in fact been in charge of a single headquarters Chief Officer, J.L. Harrington, who had in 1951 been appointed Chief Officer (Marine and Administration) of the RE, and Chief Officer (Marine and International) of the BTC in 1956. Earlier, Harrington had been Divisional Marine Manager at Dover in 1938, becoming General Assistant to the SR General Manager in 1941. At nationalisation he became one of the three 'staff officers' concerned with central policy reporting direct to Missenden, until he concentrated upon the shipping and international side. His record of continuous office was to be remarkable; he remained in the chief shipping post until 1969 when he retired as General Manager, British Rail Shipping and International Service, though continuing to serve as Deputy Chairman of the SIS Board for another couple of years.

Despite Harrington's great ability and experience, there were still occasional mutterings at Commission level that shipping should be run by shipping men. A compromise was reached when a well-known figure in shipping circles, D.F. Martin-Jenkins, was added to the Shipping Sub-Commission in 1954. However, the Shipping Sub-Commission quietly disappeared after a few years.

Meanwhile the changing nature of the market was being

reflected in the types of new vessel entering the fleet. Three new 'Dukes', for the Heysham-Belfast service originally developed by the Midland Railway, came into service in 1956. These were 21-knot ships of nearly 4,800 tons; in that year, partly as a result of a long-range study of future demand and vessel types completed in 1955, there were no less than 19 ships either under construction or ordered. A sign of the times was the commissioning of new cargo vessels designed for container traffic, the MV *Isle of Ely* on the Harwich routes and the MV *Container Enterprise* and the MV *Container Venturer* for the Irish services. By 1958 the car ferries to the Continent were reported as being fully loaded at peak periods, and addtional capacity was required. The SS *Maid of Kent* arrived for the Dover-Boulogne services, with drive-on drive-off facilities.

In 1961 the first of the modern 'general-purpose' ships came into service, the *Caledonian Princess* for the Stranraer-Larne route. This vessel was at once a passenger ship with accommodation for up to 1,400 people, and a 'drive-on, drive-off' ferry for 103 cars or 29 lorry trailers and 53 cars. Over the years the design of ships was to follow this precedent, with more and more space assigned to road vehicles.

In 1963 one of the last 'conventional' passenger ships to be built was commissioned, the SS *Avalon* for the Harwich-Hook of Holland night service. But in the same year the SS *Normannia* was converted to a car ferry for the Dover-Boulogne route and the SS *Falaise* to provide the first-ever drive-on, drive-off facilities on the Newhaven-Dieppe route. When she was joined by the MV *Villandry* and MV *Valençay* (under the French flag) Newhaven became a major vehicle ferry terminal.

In 1966 the Board decided to enter hovercraft operations and formed a subsidiary company operating under the name of 'Seaspeed' — initially with a service to the Isle of Wight.

In the same year a major step was taken, which had been in contemplation for some time, namely the concentration of the Shipping and Internatonal Services management in a central department instead of being carried out in the Regions with only co-ordination and overall policy being supplied by headquarters. The changeover took some time, the new physical concentration of staff having to wait until the new headquarters accommodation at Liverpool Street, London — the former Eastern Region offices — could be made available and adapted. Harrington became General Manager of the entire business, thoughat Board level one Member was designated to deal with the major policy aspects, an arrangement that was modified when a 'Shipping and International Services Board' was constituted in 1969 on Harrington's retirement from the General Managership (though as mentioned earlier he continued for a time as Deputy Chairman of the new Board, which had as its General Manager the shrewd Jan Posner).

By 1971 the expansion in the shipping services had been remarkable. BR had joined with with other operators on the short sea routes in a consortium with a new trading name — 'Sealink'. The BR services had always been closely associated with those of the French Railways, the Belgian Marine and the Zeeland Shipping Company; the association now became more formalised in Sealink. In 1972 Sealink carried more than six million passengers on Continental routes for the first time. New all-purpose ships, the MV *Hengist* and MV *Horsa*, helped to boost the journeys of accompanied cars to 867,000. New terminals at Folkestone, Harwich (Parkeston Quay) and Fishguard were all evidence of BR's faith in Sealink's future.

The Hovercraft company had now also established itself as an important cross-Channel carrier and the comfort and reliability of the services improved, even though, in 1970, bad weather caused 14 per cent of scheduled flights to be cancelled.

The end of the first 25 years since nationalisation coincided with a strong likelihood that a Channel Tunnel would be built in the 1970s. However, traffic on the BR sea services was so buoyant that this possibility was not allowed to inhibit the modernisation of terminals or the ordering of new ships. The modern general-purpose ships wuld have been easily redeployed on other services — to Ireland, the Channel Isles or to Holland — if the Tunnel had been built.

The two comparatively static elements in the tale of overall expansion were the train-ferry wagon services from Harwich to Dover to the Continent and the 'classic' passengers using train-and-ship services for throughout journeys. Roll-on, roll-off lorry freight was the main competitor in the former case; air travel in the latter. But overall the shipping services had never failed to show a profit, first to the British Transport Commission and latterly to the British Railways Board. Railwaymen could look enviously upon this record.

Chapter 20

How Travellers Fared

Travellers-Fare (that artificially hearty, slightly 'olde-worlde' trading name, faintly reminiscent of the ill-fated 'tavern cars' of 1949) was a title that by 1972 had not yet been applied to rail catering. The four main line railways had all had Hotels Departments which also supervised the station refreshment rooms and train catering, usually by direct management but sometimes contracted out. On nationalisation all these activities were placed under a Hotels Executive of the British Transport Commission. With the abolition of Executives in 1953, this activity became a Division of the BTC and in 1962, with the abolition of the Commission, it was re-formed as a subsidiary company of the British Railways Board, called British Transport Hotels Ltd.

At nationalisation, the railways had brought into the ownership of the BTC no less than 54 hotels, 44 in operation and 10 (partly as a result of war conditions) closed. There were also 410 station refreshment rooms — 243 operated, 157 leased to tenants, and 10 closed. There were no less than 631 locomotive-hauled restaurant cars, as well as various types of catering vehicle permanently coupled in Southern Region electric multiple-unit electric trains.

The story of the hotels is so separate from that of the railway proper that no attempt even to summarise it will be made here. But rail catering has been an interesting if chequered story.

In the early 1950s the restaurant cars were struggling, despite food rationing, to return to something like the pre-war standards. The service of full meals still predominated; in 1949 11,800,000 meals were served — the prices on regular services being 5s (25p) for breakfast, 6s (30p) for lunch and also

179

for dinner. But prices were already having to be raised, even though the possibility of operating the cars profitably remained remote.

That year saw the faintly humorous episode of the tavern cars. Oliver Bulleid of the Southern Region, always a bold innovator, designed eight sets of catering vehicles intended to run in two-coach units and incorporating sections described as resembling an old English tavern with leaded light windows and an (imitation) oak-beamed ceiling. The crowning touch was imitation brickwork painted on the exterior panels with 'hanging' inn signs such as *The Green Man* and *The Jolly Tar.* Not altogether surprisingly, this rather absurd venture was heavily criticised and did not survive long.

By 1951 a change in the character of the service was already being foreshadowed. In that year 114 full restaurant car services were replaced by the service of light refreshments, a process that was to continue almost uninterruptedly into the 1970s. Originally this new type of catering had to be provided with the existing restaurant cars although some were adapted into what were called 'cafeteria' cars, but the Hotels Executive was already considering the design of buffet cars to replace them. Buffet cars showing many variations in design, some quite successful and some less so, were to be built or adapted in quantity until the production of Mark I coaches came to an end in the early 1960s. Experiments were made with seating expressly designed to be relative uncomfortable, so that as soon as passengers had consumed their food and drink, they would be induced to move elsewhere in the train and make room for other customers. A trial was also made of cars in which the passenger accommodation was virtually windowless, again reducing its attractiveness in an attempt to shorten the time spent by customers. Not surprisingly, both these designs were so much disliked by the public that they were not perpetuated.

As the 1960s approached, the British Transport Commission admitted that many of the older restaurant cars were quite out of date, and in 1958 orders were placed for 23 restaurant cars,

38 restaurant-buffet cars and 27 kitchen-buffet cars as part of the modernisation programme. Unfortunately these still had to be basically of Mark I design. A 'griddle' car was introduced soon afterwards for an experimental period, and there was some standardisation of catering on principal trains, with a kitchen-buffet car coupled to an (unclassed) open vehicle, serving full meals from the kitchen, and drinks and light refreshments at the buffet-bar. Another feature of this period was the introduction of the 'miniature buffet' on lightly loaded services, staffed by a single attendant, and serving only drinks and snacks.

Very soon after nationalisation, the Hotels Executive took over the catering on the Southern Region (Western section) restaurant cars from Frederick Hotels Ltd. But on both the Southern and the Regions which had succeeded the former LNER, there were contracts with the Pullman Car Company that had some years to run. Pullman was still a privately-owned company that had escaped nationalisation, although it had traditionally had close links with both the Cie Internationale des Wagons-Lits and Thomas Cook & Son; its Chairman in 1948 was Stanley Adams, then Chairman of Cooks. After the Pullman Company's head office in Victoria Station was burnt out by enemy action during the war, it was temporarily housed in Cook's head office in Berkeley Street.

The Pullman cars that had been stored during the war were gradually brought back into service from 1946 onwards, until something close to the pre-war total of services had been restored. On the Southern, the 'Golden Arrow' Continental express, the 'Bournemouth Belle', and the electric mutliple-unit 'Brighton Belle' were joined in 1948 by the 'Thanet Belle', later renamed the 'Kentish Belle'. The individual Pullman cars in the electric main-line train sets — 20 sets coded as 6PUL and three as 6CIT — were supplemented by Southern pantry and buffet car sets, staffed by the Pullman Company, of which there were 17 coded as 6PAN and 13 coded as 4BUF. In addition there were the six cars built to the restricted loading gauge for the Hastings service, until replaced by multiple-unit diesels with buffet cars in 1957-58. Pullman cars also ran in the ordinary Continental expresses from Victoria, and in the ocean liner services from Waterloo.

A notable addition to Southern Pullman trains was the 'Devon Belle' inaugurated shortly before nationalisation, between Waterloo and Plymouth/Ilfracombe, with rear-end observation car. It only lasted until 1955, not having been a financial success.

On the ex-LNER services, the 'Yorkshire Pullman' had returned to service as soon after the end of the war as 1946 and the 'Queen of Scots' from King's Cross soon after nationalisation, in July 1948. Three months later a new train, the 'Tees-Tyne Pullman' was introduced. It included the then fashionable bar in one coach, the 'Hadrian Bar'.

Pullman services had not previously appeared on the Great Western Railway apart from the short-lived 'Torbay Pullman' in 1924 and Pullman-style GW saloons on Ocean Liner Specials, and it was therefore a distinct innovation when in 1955 an all-Pullman train was introduced between Paddington, Cardiff and Swansea, entitled the 'South Wales Pullman'. It was eventually displaced by the diesel multiple-unit 'Blue Pullmans' in 1961.

Reference has already been made to the regrettable side-effects of introducing the diesel 'Blue Pullman' on the London Midland Region, which considerably accelerated the process of assimilating the Pullman services into those of BR train catering. In 1954 the British Transport Commission had bought up the Ordinary share capital of the Pullman Car Company for £700,000. The investment was a good one; after the wartime suspension, dividends had again been paid from 1949 and had reached 15 per cent in 1953. The Preference shares remained in private hands for the time being.

For a time the Pullman Company was left under independent management; by 1959 it owned a fleet of 195 cars and it worked, under contract with BR, no less than 64 restaurant, buffet or pantry cars that were in BR ownership. Its profit in that year reached the record figure of £83,000. But even so the

BTC had cracked the whip to some extent; the pre-war contracts with the Southern Railway and the LNER were brought together in a new contract with the BTC in 1953, but this the Commission would not prolong beyond 1962, which effectively inhibited the Pullman Company from investing in building new cars on a large scale, though many of the older vehicles were remodelled in the Company's workshops at Preston Park, Brighton. New cars ordered in 1960 used the BR standard bodyshell.

In 1962 the Preference shares were purchased by the BTC and the Pullman Company then became a wholly owned subsidiary, first of the Commission and then of the new British Railways Board. In the following year it was announced that the Pullman operations would be 'integrated' with those of British Transport Hotels, and the virtual end of the distinctive Pullman service could be foreseen. In 1966 however there were still eleven routes upon which Pullman trains were operated, including three by the 'Blue Pullmans', but the decline thereafter was steady, and by 1972 little remained except the Manchester and Liverpool trains on the London Midland Region, scarcely differing from the regular services except for the slightly more elaborate meal service.

Many regretted the run-down of Pullman services, though admittedly heavy investment in replacement vehicles would have been necessary to keep them in their original character after the 1960s. Comparisons depend much on subjective attitudes, but it can be said that BR's restaurant car services have always been variable — some very good, others leaving a lot to be desired. The key factor has been the personality of the chief steward or conductor. But this is just where Pullman always scored in maintaining a uniform standard of service. The famous 'luxury' of their cars may have been rather dated and Edwardian; the table-lamps, the panelling and the armchairs had a period charm, but the older vehicles were beginning to ride pretty badly. The beloved 'Brighton Belle' after so many years of battering up and down the Brighton line was really something of a bone-shaker at speed! Yet one could be certain of the kind of personal service that men used to enjoy in famous West End Clubs. It turned upon the close supervision by Pullman Inspectors, the careful selection and above all the status of the Pullman conductors, who trained their staff to attend to detail in a way that the larger organisation of BR found hard to match. A factor in the Pullman tradition was the personal knowledge of the key men on the trains by the top management, and the pride in standards of service that was communicated to all the staff. The disappearance of Pullman standards of train catering comprised one element in (to use a vivid phrase coined later on by Sir Peter Parker) 'the crumbling edge of quality'.

The restaurant cars of BR always lost money, though Pullman operated at a profit. One may doubt whether the difference was wholly represented by the Pullman supplementary fare, since Pullman's expenditure on car maintenance (above the underframe), reconstruction, depreciation, etc, amounted to a very considerable charge. The secret may have resided in the closer managerial control which a smaller, tightly-knit organisation could exercise.

The refreshment rooms, unlike the restaurant cars, operated at a profit, albeit a modest one. Even so, they traditionally seemed to take second place to the restaurant cars in management attention. They were the 'down-market' end of the business; around them there still lingered the flavour of music-hall jokes about railway sandwiches, and echoes of Dickens's horror tale of Mugby Junction. The Hotels Superintendents of the pre-nationalisation companies were certainly much more interested in the more glamorous and profitable side of their departments' activity, the great business and resort hotels.

However, the LNER had established a precedent. During the war, the railways had been required to provide canteens in many places where they had not previously existed. To organise this work, the company had recruited an outside catering expert, E.K. Portman-Dixon. His success had so impressed the top management that at the end of the war he was placed in charge of the refreshment rooms throughout the system, reporting to the Chief General Manager instead of to the Area Managers through the Area Hotels Superintendents. P-D, as he was universally known, was a man of great energy and an innovator. He established a much-needed training school for refreshment room staff in a basement in Marylebone station. He tried very hard, in face of rationing and acute shortages of suitable staff, to improve the quality of service as well as the variety of food and drink. His efforts were sufficiently appreciated for him to be designated in 1948 the Refreshment Room Superintendent in the new Hotels Executive formed after nationalisation.

Here the independence he had formerly enjoyed on the LNER no longer prevailed; the traditional pre-eminence of the hotels business was re-established. Portman-Dixon, although greatly respecting the ability of his hotelier colleagues in their professional sphere, found the centralised administration of the Executive, based on the practice of the former LMS Hotels Department, hampering. However, his energy and enterprise led to his being appointed, in 1953, Chief of Restaurant Cars and Refreshment Rooms, a post which he held until retirement in 1969.

During this time many changes took place in the refreshment rooms but the most difficult problem of all remained the recruitment of suitable staff. Many rooms were modernised attractively; welcome innovations took place in widening the range of food and drink; but the standard turned more on the human element than anything else. The high rate of labour turnover and the provisions of the Catering Wages Act made local management's task extremely difficult, despite the presence of what one might imagine to be an almost captive market of rail passengers. This was by no means always an advantage, since the train timetable dictated the number of potential customers, and the consequent fluctuations in demand paid no regard to licensing hour restrictions, or availability of staff to work 'unsocial hours'. As has almost always been the case, a really efficient manager or manageress, coupled with a willing staff, was the only recipe for success.

The 'modernisation' of refreshment rooms was in some cases directed up-market, and refurbished rooms were transformed into an approximation of the 'bistro' with varying degress of success largely again depending on the staff quality, the outstanding example being the Europa Bistro at Liverpool Street station. In other stations there was a definite down-market trend, with juke-boxes and gambling machines designed to attract the young with spending power but driving away many regular travellers.

The loss of station dining rooms of the traditional type was regretted by many. The Surrey Room at Waterloo, the station dining rooms at Marylebone and Newcastle are just a few of the excellent middle-class railway restaurants that have disappeared, replaced as a rule by cafeterias.

Chapter 21
London Rail Planning

Few things illustrate more vividly the gap between the dreams of planners and the hard realities of achievement than the story of London rail planning since the war. Most of that planning, of course, primarily affected London Transport. But the main line railways have been the subject of some interesting and drastic proposals, few of which have materialised. So far as the commuter is concerned, the great improvements have come from straightforward electrification works. In the first decade after nationalisation these mainly were carried out to improve the Eastern Region services from Liverpool Street and Fenchurch Street.

The narrative must begin during the war, when post-war planning began to get under way with the 1943 County of London Plan (usually described as the Forshaw/Abercrombie Report), which really ignored the unfinished railway works from the 1935-40 New Works Programme of the main line railways and London Transport that had been 'frozen' during the war period. Instead it threw out far-reaching but very superficial proposals for cross-London rail links and major changes in the main line termini. For instance, the Plan airily proposed that:

> on reconstruction, Euston might include the facilities of St Pancras; Paddington might be enlarged and the frontage brought forward and at Liverpool Street the present site might be utilised for an underground station for suburban lines, with a new main line station accommodated on the site of the present Bishopsgate Goods station, and connected by a low level loop with a new station replacing the present Fenchurch Street station .... the riverside stations at Charing Cross, Cannon Street and Blackfriars might be replaced by underground stations below their present

187

site and the three connected on an underground system which continues from Charing Cross to Victoria Station and thence under the river to Battersea connecting to the south-western surface system; from Cannon Street it continues to Shadwell Junction, turning south under the river, via a duplicated tunnel to connect up with the south-eastern surface lines at Deptford.

This north bank loop would be supplemented by a deep-level link from Charing Cross to London Bridge via Waterloo Junction (sic). We visualise Waterloo Station remaining for a considerable time until a new station, south of the present site, would give facilities for a separate low-level connection with London Bridge .... a north-south underground connection to replace the Holborn, Blackfriars, Herne Hill route is also suggested.

These light-hearted (and unbelievably costly) proposals were submitted by J.H. Forshaw, Architect to the London County Council, and Professor Patrick Abercrombie, Professor of Town Planning in the University of London, in a massive volume commended to the public in a Foreword by Lord Latham, Chairman of the LCC, and a future Chairman of London Transport.

In the following year a Greater London Plan was published, the sole author being Professor Abercrombie, which dealt with the outer areas. Its railway proposals were virtually confined to electrification of all the remaining non-electrified commuter routes of the railways into London, and the linking up of various branches so as to provide an outer ring railway from Watford to Chelmsford, the economics and real justification for which were not properly established.

Progress from the cloud-cuckoo land of planners trained as architects, lacking any transport experience, towards more realistic forms of planning, came in stages. In February 1944 the Minister of War Transport appointed the Railway (London Plan) Committee, to investigate and report upon the transport proposals of the 1943 County of London Plan. This Committee reported in January 1946 and again in March 1948. It based its proposals on a review of pre-war needs for additonal passenger facilities; however, it accepted the dubious proposition of the Forshaw/Abercrombie Report that the Southern Railway terminals north of the river should be removed on aesthetic or broad planning principles. What emerged was a vast proposed network of new deep-level tunnels, some of 12ft (Underground 'tube') diameter, some of 17ft diameter and capable of taking main line rolling stock, connecting the principal routes north of the Thames at various places either with important traffic objectives or connections with the Southern Railway to the south of the river. In January 1946 the estimated cost of these works was put at about £230 millions.

All these proposals fell with a thump upon the desk of the Chairman of the BTC almost as soon as nationalisation was accomplished. Hurcomb was of course extremely conscious of the legacy of unfinished works in the London area, weighing upon both British Railways and London Transport, from the pre-war 1935-40 New Works Programme. He therefore followed traditional civil service practice by setting up under his own Chairmanship a small high-level committee (of which I was Secretary) to review these schemes. This body remitted the task of preparing a detailed report to a Working Party of BR and London Transport, under the chairmanship of Barrington-Ward, the Secretary being the brilliant David McKenna of London Transport, in later years General Manager of the Southern Region and eventually a Member of the British Railways Board.

The Working Party's Report owed much to McKenna's drafting skill. It was so clear and persuasive that Hurcomb sent it direct to the Minister, who published it, together with Hurcomb's covering letter, as a White Paper in 1949. The proposals modified those of the earlier reports in many respects but still proposed three passenger tubes of main line diameter, totalling 34 route miles; five passenger tubes of 'Underground' diameter, totalling 63¼ miles, and one freight tube of main line size, 5½ miles — making a total of 102¾ miles of new deep-level tunnel under London. In addition, various widenings, electrification of surface lines and other improvements were suggested.

Hurcomb's covering letter to the Minister said, very wisely, that priorities must be determined in view of the vast total expenditure envisaged. First priority should be given to Route 'C' — a new tube from the Tottenham/Edmonton area via Finsbury Park, King's Cross, Euston, Oxford Circus, Victoria, Brixton and Streatham to East Croydon.

The other first priority was Route 'D' from Hackney Downs via Liverpool Street, Bank, Ludgate Circus, Aldwych and Trafalgar Square to Victoria. Next in priority came Route 'E', a tube of main line size, connecting Southern Region electric services from Hither Green via Fenchurch Street, Bank, Trafalgar Square and Marylebone, to link up at Neasden with the services to High Wycombe, Aylesbury and (via a new junction at Kenton) with those to Berkhamstead, which would first have to be electrified.

Over a quarter of a century later, only Route 'C' has been completed, as the Victoria Line (cut back to Brixton), and a modified central portion combining parts of Routes 'D' and 'F' has been constructed, as Stage 1 of the Fleet, now the Jubilee Line.

So far as British Railways were concerned, these projects could be virtually ignored as at that time resources were only sufficient to cover some modest schemes of London suburban electrification, completing the handover to London Transport of some of the Liverpool Street suburban lines, leading to London Transport's electrification of the Eastern Region tracks between Loughton and Epping in 1949, and from Epping to Ongar in 1957. Electrification of the former LNER branch from Finsbury Park through Stroud Green and Crouch End to Highgate and Alexandra Palace was abandoned and the line closed after a review of the traffic prospects, as was the case with London Transport's proposed extensions of the Northern Line beyond Edgware and Mill Hill East.

The hard realities of the post-war world in fact forced ambitious schemes of capital expenditure to be shelved, most of them permanently. These included nearly all the Working Party's proposals for London, although London Transport

Right: The New Look in uniforms – mid 1960s: an inspector calls. (*British Rail*).

Below: One of the most handsome ships ever built for BR: SS *Avalon* for the Harwich–Hook of Holland route, with the BR reversed totem on the funnel but *not* the disfiguring SEALINK lettering on her side. (*British Rail*)

Above: The shape of things to come: APT–E on the special test track at Old Dalby about 1970. (*British Rail*). *Below:* Postscript: BR's only surviving steam train service, the Vale of Rheidol narrow-gauge line; a train approaches Devil's Bridge in 1963. (*T.J. Edgington*)

continued to press for authority to start construction of Route 'C' which was not obtained until 1962. A review of cross-London freight services was however undertaken in connection with the Modernisation Plan.

However, a substantial development came with the electrification in 1960 of the former Metropolitan & Great Central line from Harrow-on-the-Hill as far as Amersham and Chesham. BR trains from Marylebone ceased to call at most of the intermediate stations served by London Transport, and London Transport finally abandoned its Aylesbury trains, which had been steam-hauled north of Rickmansworth, in 1961.

An important cross-London link, the 'Widened Lines' of the former Metropolitan Railway between King's Cross and Moorgate, saw reduced passenger services and the gradual extinction of the freight trains that formerly used them to reach Blackfriars Bridge and the Southern Region. The reduction in wagon-load freight, coupled with the severe restriction upon the length of trains using this formerly busy route, led to cross-London freight being progressively diverted to either the West London line between Willesden Junction, North Pole Junction and Clapham Junction, or to the North and South Western Junction route via Acton Wells. The other cross-London freight route, the East London Railway, was also in disuse because of its operating disadvantages, a reversal in Liverpool Street passenger station or the use of a wagon hoist from surface to tunnel level.

A temporary stimulus to London rail planning was given by the proposal to establish a third London Airport at Maplin in Essex. Planning for the fast electrified rail connection with London involved the selection of the terminal. At one time it was proposed to double-deck either St Pancras or King's Cross, partly in order to accommodate the Airport trains, partly to enable the other stations to be closed, resulting in substantial economies. The favoured solution was the use of King's Cross. Fast electric trains would have covered the 56 miles to Maplin in about three-quarters of an hour. The cancellation of the Maplin project led to the end of this re-thinking of the future of the two great stations in the Euston Road that have glared at each other for over a century, their two clocks by tradition never agreeing to show the same time. They seem to offer a derisive comment upon the activities of the planners!

If physical new works in the 1960s were small in comparison with the far-reaching proposals of the 1948 Working Party, there was no shortage of paper work, the creation of committees and the production of reports, most of which led to little tangible progress. The constant changes in Government policy towards nationalised transport, set out in successive Acts of Parliament, did not help much. The 1962 Transport Act required BR and London Transport to co-operate in order to ensure that their services in the London Passenger Transport Area were properly 'co-ordinated', whatever that may mean! Dutifully, BR and the LT Board set up a Passenger Transport Planning Committee for London, which, following the precedent of 1948, established a Working Party. This body in 1965 produced a 'Rail Plan for London' which was still-born because yet another major Government White Paper was pending; but this, when published in 1966, merely announced *more* paper studies — a London Transportation Study, to be associated with the parallel work of a new Transport Co-ordinating Council for London. This London Transportation Study, it is noteworthy, virtually ignored public transport, being concerned with highways and traffic management for the most part!

The next non-event was a series of detailed studies of inter-change facilities at half a dozen London stations, with a survey of station car parking, produced by a Sub-Committee of the Transport Co-ordinating Council. In 1969 the Greater London Council set up a Greater London Transport Group to replace the Transport Co-ordinating Council for London, and this body at last included BR representatives.

The main benefit in terms of physical improvements from all these statutes, committees and reports came from the provisions of the 1968 Transport Act which enabled the Government to make 'infrastructure grants' for the improvement of passenger services. The two important results, so far as London was concerned, were grants for the Great Northern suburban electrification on the Eastern Region (King's Cross and Moorgate to Welwyn Garden City, Hertford North, Stevenage and Royston) on the BR side, and for the first stage of the London Transport Fleet Line, renamed the Jubilee Line at the instance of the GLC, not altogether happily in view of its snail-like progress towards completion. The principle of infrastructure grants did however benefit BR through help with, for example, London Bridge re-signalling in 1971 and new Southern Region rolling stock.

But, looking back from 1972 over the 25 years since nationalisation, one is bound to feel that the actual achievements in London Rail Planning have been extraordinarily ineffective compared with what has been achieved in cities such as Paris or Montreal and many others overseas, and even in provincial Britain. The 1968 Transport Act which set up Passenger Transport Executives in the provincial 'conurbations' led to the launching of 'Merseyrail' and the new 'Metro' in Tyne and Wear, for instance, so why then has London lagged behind? Why, when BR has worked in partnership, (effectively, despite some initial differences with PTEs) on Merseyside and Tyneside to improve local transport, has so little appeared in the Metropolis? Before the war, the Standing Joint Committee of the four main line railways and the London Passenger Transport Board achieved a great deal in the way of co-ordinated development. Since the war, progress has been poor by comparison.

A question that is sometimes asked is whether the relationship between BR and the Greater London Council need be different from those between BR and the provincial PTEs. Would a more efficient public service be provided if BR's suburban services were financed (and thereby controlled) by the GLC? But the arguments against this are weighty. Relatively few BR suburban services fall entirely within the

GLC area. One might instance the North London line from Broad Street to Richmond, but even here there is inter-working with peak hour services from Broad Street to Watford in Hertfordshire, while the Southern Region 'inner suburban' services share the use of staff and assets with outer suburban and even some long-distance services. The latter situation led, in the days between 1969 and 1974 when separate grants were made for individual 'socially necessary' rail services, to the Southern Region services in London and the South-East being treated as a unit for financial assessment purposes. And, it must be said, relations between the GLC and London Transport since 1969, when LT came under GLC control, have not been so happy as to suggest that BR would enjoy a good relationship with the local authority.

So this study ends rather depressingly in 1972. It must be added that subsequently, however, some major proposals have emerged. One that was frustrated (by a Government reneging on a commitment to the Channel Tunnel) was for a Tunnel passenger terminal at the White City connecting with the proposed high-speed line from London to the Tunnel. Others that have subsequently taken shape have been for a massive interchange at West Hampstead between the (elect-rified) Midland suburban line, the North London line, and London Transport's Jubilee Line. There is renewed interest in orbital schemes based on minor investment in new connect-ions between existing stretches of route, and North-South through services. So perhaps there is hope for modest improve-ments to London's rail facilities despite the stagnation of so many years.

Chapter 22

The Workshops Story

Before 1939, the railway workshops had not markedly changed since the pre-grouping era when almost every railway possessed its own locomotive, carriage and wagon shops, and all the major railways — and some minor ones — built as well as maintained their engines and rolling stock. Minor changes of course took place under the grouping, in particular some concentration of new construction and some cutting down at the smaller establishments. For instance, Stoke-on-Trent and Kilmarnock Works were closed by the LMS. But, in the main, Crewe, Derby, Swindon, Wolverton, Doncaster, Darlington, Eastleigh and Ashford kept their traditional status as railway towns, as did a host of other centres.

During the war the shops came under the unified control of the Railway Executive Committee's Mechanical Engineers' Committee, and two things happened. New building was drastically reduced; much shop capacity was diverted from railway work to producing war materials, and where necessary, the remaining capacity was used to meet railway needs arising anywhere, not merely on the owning company's system.

There were of course limits to this 'common user' practice. Stocks of spares, drawing office records and, above all, experience and 'know-how' favoured maintenance being generally confined to the owning company's stock. But there were new non-company designs — the 2-8-0 'Austerity' freight locomotives, and the MWT 16-ton mineral wagons, for instance — which had no such affiliations.

With nationalisation, and unified control on a permanent rather than a temporary wartime basis, a national workshops policy became both desirable and possible. For the time being, however, the workshops were left under the Regional

Chief Mechanical and Electrical Engineers and changes, pending the delayed appearance of a real British Railways traction policy, were not very marked. It was a period of shortages and arrears of maintenance; the need to catch up the wartime backlog and to inject new building into the run-down stocks was paramount. Although the Railway Executive intended from the start to build new standard BR steam locomotives, for the time being it was essential to continue the construction of company designs to the full extent that investment restrictions would permit. This meant using the capacity of Regional workshops to build company types with which they were familiar, and also continuing the pre-war practice of drawing substantially upon the resources of the outside locomotive building industry. The extent to which this took place is shown by the following table:

	Deliveries of new locomotives		
	Railway shops	Contractors	Total
1948	314	96	410
1949	301	95	396
1950	311	103	414
1951	278	63	341
1952	237	62	299

Contractors were also used extensively for coaching vehicles.

	New coaching stock construction		
	Railway shops	Contractors	Total
1948	844	490	1,334
1949	1,297	504	1,801
1950	2,367	352	2,719
1951	1,513	410	1,923
1952	675	329	1,004

But by far the most extensive use of outside builders was for wagons. The following table shows construction over the first five years.

	Freight vehicles (excluding service vehicles)		
	Railway shops	Contractors	Total
1948	18,690	20,477	39,167
1949	14,934	16,676	31,610
1950	14,798	12,908	27,706
1951	15,580	21,330	36,910
1952	10.097	17,792	27,889

As early as 1948, boilers and other components were being repaired or manufactured on an inter-Regional basis and by 1949 Derby was repairing pannier tank engines for Swindon and J39s for the Eastern Region. By 1951, the first of the BR standard steam locomotive classes was in production, all at railway shops. But the move towards a real national workshops policy was at first hesitant. There was on the one hand a strong presumption that the total capacity of BR shops, if fully re-planned and rationalised, ought to be sufficient to enable outside contractors to be dispensed with, at any rate in the case of locomotives. It was not so clear whether carriage replacements could all be provided from BR shops; and for the time being a large number of private wagon builders and repairers would continue to be needed, although the Railway Executive made a start in withdrawing some repair work from them early on.

The gradual run-down in building locomotives to pre-nationalisation designs, and the build-up in construction of new BR standard types, led to a concentration of work upon the railway shops which had some serious consequences for the private locomotive manufacturers. With steam traction progressively disappearing in the export markets, and British Railways determined to be practically self-sufficient in steam locomotive construction, the industry faced a bleak prospect unless it could convert quickly to producing diesel or electric locomotives. This would involve, at least, sharing of work between BR and the industry; there was no prospect of BR embarking upon the manufacture of diesel engines, electric motors or electrical control gear, (though the electrical engineers had rated highly the motors built in the L&Y days at Horwich for the Manchester-Bury electric stock!). But the delay in the appearance of substantial orders for diesel engines meant that the private industry faced sharp contraction, until the Modernisation Plan of 1955 produced a flood of orders for both railway workshops and private firms, initially for diesel multiple-unit vehicles and prototype main line diesel loco-motives, at long last following up the pioneer work of H.G.

Ivatt on the LMS with his introduction of the quite successful prototypes, Nos 10000 and 10001.

The building of standard steam locomotives in BR shops was tapered off, to finish in 1959/60, years which showed deliveries of diesel locomotives coming to a peak, as the following table shows.

	Deliveries of new diesel locomotives		
	Railway shops	Contractors	Total
1959	328	273	601
1960	350	401	751

Contractors were being used on a large scale for the construction of wagons (41,565 in 1956, for instance) and for coaching vehicles (748 in the same year). But it was a sign of changing times that in the Annual Report for 1960 the BTC warned that it had always been its policy 'to carry out repairs to locomotives and other rolling stock in their own workshops, and to manufacture in these shops equipment and components for which they are already laid out, provided that their costs remain competitive .... with the introduction of modern types of motive power and other rolling stock, numbers in existing fleets will decline, and there will be fewer orders for replacements and repairs in the future. Consequently a gradual run-down in railway workshops capacity was foreseen at the same time as reduced orders to manufacturers and wagon repairers.' In pursuit of the new policy, in 1962 locomotive construction at Horwich was discontinued, as was wagon construction at Faverdale and Lancing, and coaching stock building at Eastleigh, Swindon and Wolverton.

But it was only with the setting-up of the British Railways Board that a truly new Workshops policy emerged, in 1963. The plan set up a new central management, removing the shops from Regional control, and a complete rationalisation of facilities involving the closure of some shops and the improvement and modernisation of those that were to contunue. Main Works were initially to be reduced in number from 28 to 16, with a corresponding reduction in staff numbers, then around 62,000.

The key figure in producing the Workshops Plan was Sir Steuart Mitchell, who had joined the British Transport Commission in February 1962 after long experience in controlling naval dock-yards and workshops. Sir Steuart became Vice-Chairman of the British Railways Board and initiated a programme of major reorganisation. The run-down of steam was already enabling a concentration of repair work at particular shops to be effected. All steam repairs were withdrawn from Derby, Doncaster and St Rollox (Glasgow), Horwich and Wolverhampton. New carriage construction was concentrated at Derby and York, with Wolverton devoted to the repair of locomotive-hauled stock and electric multiple-units.

A review of the workshops showed that many of them, having been constructed (in some cases over 100 years ago) for steam locomotive practice, and starved of adequate funds for maintenance and rebuilding, were unsuited to meet modern requirements. Staff amenities urgently needed improvement at many places.

A new practice was instituted, of inviting competitive tenders from the Workshops and the outside manufacturers. The two processes of closure on the one hand and investment on the other, continued, the outlay on modernisation running to over £16 million. As the plan proceeded, emphasis shifted to the purchase of new machine tools. The Workshops Plan was finally completed during 1967, by which year, with the Beeching Re-shaping virtually complete, the construction of locomotives and rolling stock presented a very different picture from that of ten years earlier, as the figures show:

	New building		
Year 1967	Railway shops	Contractors	Total
Locomotives	15	45	60
Coaching vehicles			
(loco-hauled, emu, dmu)	370	112	482
Freight wagons	1,590	nil	1,590

The transformation in the pattern of new building, compared with that on page 198, is dramatic.

Another great change was introduced in the Transport Act, 1968. For the first time, the Workshops were permitted to manufacture for outside industry. This had previously been outwith the statutory powers of the railways, presumably in order to protect the private manufacturers from 'unfair' competition. (In consequence, before nationalisation there had been one or two instances where locomotives had been built by one railway for another, but had needed to run for a short time on the system of the builder company, in order to be sold as ostensibly second-hand stock.)

The new position led to the setting up of a new company, British Rail Engineering Ltd, to manage the main workshops — now reduced in number to 14 — in place of the BR Workshops organisation. BREL, as it was quickly named for commercial purposes, went into business with an annual turnover of about £100 million and a staff of around 37,000 people. It started trading on 1 January 1970.

With the aim of increasing its outside commercial activities, BREL joined forces with the only major railway rolling stock manufacturer remaining in the private sector, Metro-Cammell Ltd, to set up a joint subsidiary, BRE-Metro Ltd to promote export sales of locomotives and rolling stock. Another sign of the times was that BREL became a full member of the Locomotive and Allied Manufacturers' Association, now renamed the Railway Industry Association, but representing an industry much reduced in scale from the time when British railway material had been exported on a great scale all over the world.

At the beginning of the 1970s, the recession in freight traffic and the reduction in the size of the carriage and wagon stocks had led to a considerable drop in the workload on BREL, compensated to some extent by work for outside parties, including coaches for Coras Iompair Eireann (Irish Transport Company), Northern Ireland Railways and London Transport, and 800 covered wagons for the Yugoslav Railways. The reduction in the orders from BR was a temporary phase arising from the surge in construction and purchases of locomotives and rolling stock under the Modernisation Plan, 10 to 15 years previously; and it was easy to foresee a corresponding upsurge in demand a few years ahead when much of the Plan's equipment, above all the diesel multiple-units which had been the first elements to enter service in large numbers, would fall due for replacement. So, after a quarter-century of unified ownership and some drastic slimming, the Workshops could look forward to a period when the main problem would not be that of filling the order book, but of capacity to meet both the requirements of BR and the commitments to outside customers.

Chapter 23
Channel Tunnel Episode

The Channel Tunnel project lay dormant for many years after the critical hour in 1930 when a motion approving its constuction was lost by only seven votes in the House of Commons. But after the 1939-45 war an important declaration was made by the British Government to the effect that there no longer could be any military or strategic objections to the Tunnel's construction, and in 1957 an influential Channel Tunnel Study Group was formed comprising the hitherto dormant British and French Channel Tunnel Companies, the Suez Finance Company and Technical Studies Inc, an American financial group.

Sir Brian Robertson, unlike his three successors, strongly supported the Channel Tunnel and in the Commission's Annual Report for 1957 made it clear that the BTC welcomed the establishment of the Study Group and would give it practical assistance. An Adviser on the General Staff was put in charge of the Channel Tunnel liaison work.

The Study Group financed a large number of borings of the sea bed and, with the assistance of economic and technical consultants, developed a project for a bored rail tunnel under the Channel which would also proved a form of 'rolling motorway' for road traffic. In addition to linking the railway systems of Britain and France, the tunnel would operate ferry trains for motor vehicles — cars, coaches and lorries — between terminals close to the British and French coasts, using rail wagons built to standards of width and height exceeding anything previously in use. The terminals would be built on a loop principle, with continuous operation by the ferry trains without reversing. The rail services for train passengers would involve interchange between Southern

Region trains and trains to the Continental loading gauge, to be effected at a station near the British tunnel portal.

The British Transport Commission, as successors to the Southern Railway Company, had inherited a substantial interest in the British Channel Tunnel Company. In 1959, contacts between the French Railways and BR were established on the railway aspects of the new tunnel project and a good many technical issues were settled. In the following year the British and French Governments were presented with the Channel Tunnel Study Group's detailed scheme, then estimated to cost about £109 million including the cost of the terminals and rolling stock, but excluding financial charges. The BTC then expressed the hope that the British Government would reach an early conclusion on the project.

The subsequent procrastination of the two Governments, above all the British, seems in retrospect, 20 years later, to have been pitiful. Three years after the Study Group's submission, the two Governments issued a White Paper drafted by civil servants who had examined the project and found it economically sound. Nothing much more happened for three more years until a second study, not this time published, was also completed by British and French civil servants broadly endorsing the conclusions of the 1963 report. At last things began to happen, and in 1966 the Prime Ministers of Great Britain and France announced a definite decision that the Tunnel should be built, subject to detailed agreements on how the work should be carried out.

One morning that year the telephone on my desk rang and Charles Haygreen, then Management Development Officer, asked me if I was prepared to add the Channel Tunnel to my existing responsibilities. I was asked to give him an answer within half an hour. It appeared that the Minister of Transport had at last appointed an Assistant Secretary to take charge of a Channel Tunnel Department, and had demanded to know who would be his opposite number in BR. An appointment therefore had to be made instantly! I agreed to take it on and began seven years' work on a project which, inherently feasible and economically well justified, was bedevilled by political jealousies and the intervention of far too many interests.

It was soon made clear to me that road transport interests had been successfully lobbying the two Governments to persuade them that the Tunnel must not be managed by the railways but on completion must be handed over to an Anglo-French Channel Tunnel Operating Authority. At the same time, the Governments wanted the Tunnel built by private finance. In consequence, the negotiations with those expected to pay for the Tunnel's construction were, to say the least, complicated.

A major setback, lasting nearly a year, occurred as the result of the civil disturbances in France in 1968. Once these had ceased to inhibit progress, the French Government decided that a fresh re-appraisal of the economics of the project must be made, and this was carried out by a French consultancy firm. Meanwhile the exchanges between BR and the SNCF continued, sometimes revealing engineering problems that needed solution, sometimes curious differences of outlook such as the argument over train lavatories. The Chief Inspecting Officer of Railways in the British Ministry of Transport was adamant that no discharge from train lavatories on to the track could be permitted in the Tunnel, for reasons of public health. The French, shrugging their shoulders, pointed out that no problems appeared to arise from this cause in other long tunnels, for instance under the Alps; were not their British colleagues being over-sensitive about hygiene?

The project nevertheless continued to lurch forward; the 1968 Transport Act provided for the setting up of a Channel Tunnel Planning Council which would constitute in 'shadow' form the British half of the future Anglo-French Channel Tunnel Operating Authority, and also empowered the Minister of Transport to acquire land for the purpose of the future Channel Tunnel terminal sites. A site for the car-ferry terminal was selected at Cheriton, behind Folkestone, and at Saltwood for the railway junction with the Southern Region main line.

Continuing the policy of wanting to have their cake and eat

it, the Governments insisted that although the Channel Tunnel Study Group had carried out such thorough planning, it could not be the designated agency for Tunnel construction; there must be competitive tendering. Invitations to tender were therefore published and after a delay of some months, three tenders were actually received from different financial groups.

Having obtained competitive tenders, the Governments found it too fatiguing to choose between them, and a request was made to the parties to consolidate their proposals in the form of a single tender! More delays, but eventually this was done with the result that a new company comprising a consortium of merchant bankers was formed in which the old Channel Tunnel Company participated. Rather confusingly, the new company was henceforth called the Channel Tunnel Company Ltd while the old company, dating from the 1880s, was renamed Channel Tunnel Investments Ltd. The British Railways Board participated in the new company while retaining its shareholding in the old one and thus had a double interest in the Tunnel.

An important development, with both advantages and disadvantages for BR, was the arrival on the scene of the Rio Tinto-Zinc Company, which took up a share in the capital of the 'chosen instrument', the new Channel Tunnel Company. RT-Z formed a subsidiary company, RT-Z Development Enterprises Ltd, to act as project managers for the British half of the Tunnel construction work. The advantages came from RT-Z's resources in planning and constructing large-scale projects such as hydro-electric schemes, mining and aluminium smelting in widely separated parts of the world; their effective methods of cost control, and the impetus which their people were able to impart whenever matters seemed to drag. The disadvantages arose from RT-Z's insistence that everything that had been done before must be re-tested and if necessary modified. When this was applied to purely railway aspects of the project, where a great amount of preliminary work had been satisfactorily completed, hackles occasionally rose!

In the event, RT-Z did not effect any fundamental change in the concept as it had been developed by the Channel Tunnel Study Group ten years earlier, though they improved it in detail and carried planning on in accordance with the demands of the timetable, experiencing with their French opposite numbers some of the differences which we in BR were accustomed to encounter with our French railway colleagues, all of which had to be removed by discussion and goodwill. The goodwill was perhaps more apparent between the British and French railwaymen than between the two project Managers!

But already by 1970 a major railway problem had arisen. The original Study Group's idea of an interchange station on the British side of the Tunnel for all rail passengers, and much freight, was considered to be an obstacle to the growth of traffic; the inconvenience of having to change trains, carrying one's luggage, and the lengthening of journey times by at least half an hour, possibly more, to allow for Customs and Immigration controls, would destroy much of the appeal of the Tunnel services. Through running to the Continent with rolling stock capable of running also in Britain, ie with restricted dimensions, similar to those of the Wagon-Lits sleeping cars in the 'Night Ferry' trains that ran between London, Paris and Brussels using the Dover-Dunquerque ferry ships, was proposed by BR. The precedent was clear.

The Continental railways objected strongly. They saw this as the thin end of a wedge which would lead to non-standard passenger coaches, including sleeping cars, knocking about at all sorts of places on the Continent, requiring special arrangements for maintenance and for return workings. They urged strongly that BR ought to enlarge the loading gauge between the Tunnel and London so as to enable trains of standard Continental stock to run non-stop from Paris or Lille to London.

A gauging exercise was accordingly carried out. It was not possible to contemplate using the No 1 boat train route between Ashford and London through Tonbridge, Sevenoaks and Dulwich because of the long tunnels (Sevenoaks, Polhill and Penge) which it would have been excessively costly to enlarge, and also because of the dislocation to the heavy existing traffic that would be involved during the work. So the secondary route from Ashford to Swanley via Maidstone East, and from Shortlands to Brixton via Catford, was studied. The cost of enlarging the clearances was found to be between £35 and £40 million and journey speeds would be lower than on the No 1 boat train route. It was therefore ruled out and the Continental railways were so informed.

The SNCF came back with a rejoinder. They were studying the design of future very high speed railways for which the code name was 'Europolitain'. The principle was this: between major cities, existing terminals and tracks in the fully built-up areas would be utilised, but once open country was reached, new high-speed tracks would be built. These would incorporate curves of exceedingly wide radius, not restricting speeds at all, but construction costs would be drastically reduced because the trains would have very high power-to-weight ratios and would therefore experience no difficulty in coping with gradients normally considered impossible for main line operation, as steep as 1 in 28. Approaching the destination city, the new line would rejoin the existing tracks. Construction costs would also be reduced because in places the 'Europolitain' lines would be twinned with a new motorway, thus saving both land usage and engineering costs.

Two schemes were under study, the French told us: one entitled 'Paris-Sud-Est', between Paris and Lyons, designed to provide extra capacity and greatly reduce journey times on the heavily-loaded routes to the second city of France, to Switzerland, the Riviera and Italy; the other, 'Paris-Nord', from Paris to Lille, Brussels and the Netherlands. Which would be given priority was still an open question. But if the Channel Tunnel were built, there could be links to it from 'Paris-Nord' and if only the British would provide a similar link on their side, dramatic reductions in rail journey times between London, Paris and Brussels could be envisaged; 2½ hours London to Paris and 2¼ hours London to Brussels would be intensely competitive with the best time possibly by air, reckoned from city centre to city centre. And, argued the French, the distance from the Tunnel to London was far less than that from Paris to the Tunnel. So where was the problem?

This was examined with some scepticism at BRB headquarters. Neither the Chairman, Sir Henry Johnson, nor his immediate predecessor, Sir Stanley Raymond, had evinced any great enthusiasm for the Channel Tunnel. But two Board Members, John Ratter and David McKenna, to whom in succession I reported, gave it full support. Permission was given to entrust the preparation of a feasibility study for a high-speed Channel Tunnel link to a firm of engineering consultants, since neither the Chief Civil Engineer at headquarters nor the Southern Region considered that they had the resources for such a task in view of their other commitments.

The consultants produced studies for four possible routes. Three of these were so obviously going to provoke violent opposition, striking across some of the most beautiful scenery in Kent, that we quickly decided to concentrate attention on the remaining one which utilised a combination of existing Southern Region routes, requiring only some widenings and new connections. It followed the No 1 boat train route from Saltwood through Ashford to Tonbridge, then the old South Eastern main line towards Redhill, diverging to join the Oxted line which it followed through South and East Croydon, then by a new tunnel joining the Crystal Palace line west of Streatham Hill, continuing by a widening of the Brighton main line as far as Clapham Junction, whence either Victoria would be reached, or a new terminal on the West London line.

This route had obvious advantages but it also raised problems, largely within the built-up area where speeds would have to be restricted. For the moment, it lay on the table as no more than what it was, a feasibility study. Both politicians and civil servants threw cold water on it whenever it was mentioned.

But the momentum of the project was increasing. It was

agreed that BR should provide the rail technical consultancy services to the project managers, and in October 1972 Agreement No 1 was signed between the British and French Governments, the British and French Channel Tunnel Companies and the financing groups which included the British and French railways. The BRB's Annual Report for 1972 contained a hopeful note (the new Chairman, Richard Marsh, was an enthusiastic supporter of the project) to the effect that Agreement No 2 should be ready for signature in July 1973, and this in fact proved to be the case.

Agreement No 2 provided the specification for the rail infrastructure between London and the Tunnel: in a sudden volte-face the Government, urged on by RT-Z (who saw the need to maximise the through rail traffic through the tunnel and not merely the road vehicle ferry), decided to support the new high-speed, high-capacity rail link. They did not foresee the final estimated cost of the project, nor the strength of opposition it would arouse.

So the first 25 years of BR's existence saw the likelihood of the Tunnel come very close indeed. Both the major political parties appeared to support it. The combination of circumstances that led to the sudden Labour Government decision to pull out in January 1975 make a fascinating study, but outside the scope of this account.

Chapter 24

The Power Game

If any politically-minded idealist (or idealistic politician) had expected in 1948 that nationalisation would lead to fewer internal stresses, less power politics than in the days of private ownership of railways, they were wide of the mark. Of course, personal rivalries and organisational changes had played their part in the former railway companies, as in all large businesses, but in the first 25 years of British Railways' existence, there were no fewer than four major Acts of Parliament, in 1947, 1953, 1962 and 1968, each drastically changing the organisation. Superimposed on these statutory changes there were internal reorganisations reflecting the views of powerful individuals, and personal power struggles which, for the most part, did little to solve the underlying difficulties which the railway industry was facing.

In the early years from 1948 to 1953, it was no secret that the British Transport Commission and the Railway Executive were often at loggerheads over the way in which the railways should be run. But, equally, there was tension between the Executive and its Chief Regional Officers who resented the directives given by Executive Members to the departmental officers in the Regions. The CROs early on formed a Committee to discuss matters of common interest, including a common front against the Executive when this seemed necessary. The Executive, hearing of this, sent a formal instruction to the CROs to discontinue such meetings, but, as a sop, invited them to attend alternate meetings of the Executive for the discussion of policy questions affecting the Regions.

Human nature being what it is, the CROs obeyed, so far as abandoning their formal meetings was concerned, but immediately replaced them with informal luncheon meetings serving the same purpose, to which it was impossible for the Executive to object without making itself ridiculous.

Rather similar manoeuvres took place between the Commission, the nominally superior body, and the Executive. The BTC wanted to keep in touch with all that was going on, and directed the RE to send in copies of the minutes of its meetings. The Executive complied, but arranged to produce two sets of Minutes. Those on white paper were supplied to the BTC, and were considerably expurgated; those on green paper, officially termed 'Memoranda of decisions', were used within the Executive as a record of what had *really* been discussed and decided. Of course, the existence of the 'green minutes' could not be kept a secret for very long.

Personal relations between the two original Chairmen, Lord Hurcomb and Sir Eustace Missenden, were not cordial. Missenden was good at 'stonewalling' to resist pressure from the Commission; Hurcomb was impatient at the slow progress being made with the 'integration' enjoined by the Transport Act, 1947.

When Sir Brian Robertson arrived to preside over the assortment of businesses, some vast in scale, which the Transport Act of 1953 had put directly under the Commission, the first reaction of the staff was that now a real leader had appeared. Sir Brian was a man of commanding presence and great integrity, expecting and receiving respect. Some mistook his icy manner (based upon shyness) for arrogance. C.K. Bird, when General Manager of the Eastern Region, once observed to some of his officers: 'The Chairman is the most fair-minded and impartial man I have ever met. He hates us all equally'. CKB's mordant wit had led him into misjudgment.

Sir Brian expected complete loyalty from those who worked with him; he did not necessarily look for intellectual brilliance. The nearest thing to a twinkle in the Chairman's eye that some of us ever saw was when, describing in military 'briefing' style the new organisation at headquarters, he remarked: 'And Sir Reginald Wilson will now become a Commission Member pure if not simple'.

Sir Reginald in fact had been immersed in power politics since nationalisation, as Comptroller of the Commission, in which capacity he had put together the finances of the BTC's oddly-assorted collection of businesses in a masterly fashion. He was the unquestioned 'financial wizard' of nationalised transport. But although Sir Brian might find RHW's views, often original and always vigorously expressed, rather hard to follow, he appreciated their quality sufficiently to appoint him Chairman of, first, the Eastern and later the London Midland Area Board, where his invigorating influence upon railway policy could be most directly exercised.

The success in the power game which Wilson enjoyed had eluded Miles Beevor, the first Chief Secretary of the British Transport Commission. Beevor, whilst still comparatively young, had come from an outside legal practice to become Chief Legal Adviser of the LNER. In that capacity he had so greatly impressed the Board that, on the retirement of Sir Charles Newton in 1947, Beevor was appointed Acting Chief General Manager (the Ministry of Transport would not agree to a substantive appointment in view of impending nationalisation). When the BTC was set up in 'shadow' form, Beevor was designated as its Chief Secretary and Legal Adviser.

In view of his previous position, he was entitled to expect that he would be the chief executive of the Commission; but that was not within Hurcomb's intentions. Beevor was not encouraged to deal with policy except as the mouthpiece of the Commission; in other words, as a Secretary and not as a General Manager. Beevor, who had high abilities — sometimes affected by his quickness and impatience — as well as a deep interest in railway matters, found this hard (ultimately impossible) to accept, particularly as Wilson seemed to have a free hand in dictating financial policy, a field which Hurcomb was willing to delegate. Beevor left, at the invitation of Sir Ronald Matthews, his former Chairman on the LNER, to become Managing Director of the Brush Electrical Engineering Company.

There was in fact for many years an open question why

neither the BTC nor BR, unlike must other businesses, had a chief executive, chief general manager or managing director. Beevor's successor was his former deputy, Sidney Taylor, who had made his previous career in the Secretary's office of the Great Western Railway and was willing to accept the purely secretarial status which had irked Beevor. After 1955, the position of Secretary-General held by Major-General Wansbrough Jones was rather jealously regarded by some, particularly in the Regions, in case 'Wansbrough' should claim to be the chief executive. In fact, Sir Brian regarded him as merely Chief of Staff and when asked by the Select Committee on Nationalised Industries if the Secretary-General was the chief executive, promptly corrected this; the Chairman was himself the chief executive — 'there was no doubt about it'.

Sir Brian had discharged the obligation to decentralise the railways by devising Area Boards; inevitably some power struggles between the Boards and the centre arose, particularly over the amount and control of investment funds for modernisation. The British Railways Central Staff were often in a difficult position. Seeking to set standards, on the one hand they might find their proposals modified or criticised by the General Staff who stood between them and the Commission; on the other, they might be subject to pressure from Regions who wanted to depart from any standards set at headquarters. Regional officers might prime the Chairman of their Area Boards to use their quite considerable weight with the Commission to secure acceptance of a Regional argument.

The classic case was of course the decision to continue to use the vacuum brake, which the Commission took in deference to Regional opinion against the recommendation of the BR Central Staff, an expensive mistake in the long run.

The complicated BTC organisation between 1955 and 1962 lent itself to lobbying and power politics; but the Chairman's personal prestige and his ability to issue statements of policy in an apparently convincing manner, coupled with Wansbrough-Jones's skill in drafting papers for the Ministry and for internal use, prevented the cracks from being too obvious, even though the Stedeford Advisory Group saw the defects of the organisation very clearly.

Sir Brian Robertson was responsible for one major innovation, the concept of a Staff College for future managers. It was not to be a slavish copy of the Army Staff College at Camberley: it had more affinities with the Administrative Staff College at Henley-on-Thames which had been initiated principally to serve private industry, though the civil service and nationalised industries also made use of it. The British Transport Commission sent one or two men to the Henley courses in most years since nationalisation.

The British Transport Staff College was set up in 1959, adapting the former Southern Railway's school at Gorse Hill, Woking by adding a new residential block and upgrading the amenities of this attractive Lutyens house. It was designed to serve three main purposes: to improve the long-term performance of the young and middle-range managers sent there; to enable men from different branches of the Commission's undertaking to get to know each other and understand each others' problems; and — very important — in the immediate future, to serve as a 'gold-fish bowl' in which any particularly promising individuals could be quickly identified and, if appropriate, given accelerated promotion. It had therefore some of the character of a forcing-house and also of a 'country house' type of selection board. The reason was that Sir Brian saw a need to improve management performance both in the short and the long term.

An echo of Camberley was felt when a soldier, Major-General W.D.A. Williams, became the first Principal. Bill Williams was the ideal man to establish quickly good relations, both with the management units within the Commission and also with the course members. He was hospitable and convivial, but also a shrewd judge of character. He delegated extensively but knew how to keep in touch with what was going on.

I was appointed the first Director of Studies and was fortunate in acquiring quickly a team of four able young Assistant Directors. We were given a free hand by Bill Williams in the construction of the early courses, where we largely followed the Henley pattern of syndicate work, using visiting lecturers rather than staff instructors, presentation of syndicate reports, conferences and overseas visits. There was at first some resistance on the part of the BTC managements to releasing promising men for as long as three months; Sir Brian's reaction (coloured by his Camberley experience) was that he wished the courses could be at least twice as long. His hope was certainly that, as in the Army, the magic letters 'psc' (passed Staff College) on a staff history sheet, in time would become essential for promotion into top management.

When the BTC was abolished a hot debate arose as to whether the Staff College should pass to the British Railways Board — in which case several of the other successor Boards of the BTC made it clear that they would no longer send their young men there — or continue to serve nationalised transport in the widest sense. The second view prevailed and the College became a company limited by guarantee, sponsored by most (though not all) of the successor Boards. In later years it steadily widened its scope, drawing course members from the Army, from overseas and private sector industry, although retaining its link with BR as its most important single sponsor.

In some respects the Staff College is Sir Brian's most enduring legacy to nationalised transport. After Sir Brian retired, organisation took a different form under Dr Beeching, who assigned to individual Board Members the control of railway functions; the elaborate headquarters structure of Committees withered away. The chief cause of possible difficulty arose when two Board Members' functions overlapped or conflicted at Regional level. There, new statutory Boards had appeared under the 1962 Act, of which General Managers tended to become the Chairmen, so that the previous occasional tensions between the GMs and their Area Board Chairmen — not unknown on one or two of the Regions — would not be perpetuated. Dr Beeching seemed to prefer to solve problems directly and not through formal institutional means, to which both Hurcomb and Robertson had been addicted.

Tensions sometimes were felt between the Beeching 'new men' and the 'regulars' of the railways. But in many cases a modus vivendi was established, and some of the 'hard-faced men' from industry identified themselves closely with their railway colleagues. In a few cases, a sigh of relief went up when the stranger within the gate decided to return to the outside world.

An interesting situation developed after Dr Beeching's departure from BR, with two such different — though forceful — characters as S.E. (Sir Stanley) Raymond and Philip Shirley as Chairman and Vice-Chairman respectively. Life at head-quarters was not exactly placid; but it changed, the atmosphere becoming more relaxed, when H.C. ('Bill') Johnson, soon to become Sir Henry, was appointed Chairman after Raymond's sudden departure.

The power game did not depend solely upon personalities but also upon ideas. Since nationalisation the railway organi-sation has so often been changed that a disproportionate amount of management time has been involved in coping with changes, together with a vast amount of personal inconvenience and frustration on the part of individuals whose careers have been dislocated. Of course, on the other side the changes have sometimes enabled unexpected ability to be discovered.

A long and unprofitable dispute over Regional boundaries dragged on until 1955. In the end, purely geographical boundaries were decided upon by the BTC, although the Regional General Managers (with one exception, the North Eastern) preferred the 'system' concept. The process of tidying up was tedious.

A much more fruitful development was one that appeared in the Eastern Region, inspired by Sir Reginald Wilson, namely the creation of smaller units with many of the character-istics of general management. These 'Lines' within the Region were three — initially the London, Tilbury & Southend, of which John Dedman made a considerable success, followed by the Great Northern under Gerard Fiennes and the Great

Eastern under W.G. Thorpe. The 'Lines' took shape as 'real railways'. Gerard Fiennes and Willie Thorpe, both dedicated operating men though very different in temperament, emerged as personalities in the eye both of the public and of their staffs. The concept was one that largely reversed the over-centralisation, the trend towards drab uniformity that had been a danger ever since nationalisation. And the risk of capricious variation in specifications for equipment was averted by headquarters reserving technical standards to itself.

Sadly, the 'Line' concept did not transplant very well. For a time it was adopted in Scotland and on the Southern. On the Western, geography made it impracticable, as was the case on the North Eastern. Sir Reginald Wilson then moved to the Chairmanship of the London Midland Region. There had been many discussions in the past about the excessive size of the Region and a study had been made soon after nationalisation about the possibility of creating a separate North Western Region based on Manchester. On the face of it, splitting the former London & North Western system off from the former Midland system would seem a more logical and effective form of decentralisation. But Euston, entrenched in the traditions of centralisation established by the LMS, defeated even Sir Reginald's reforming zeal.

In the end, the Lines were abolished everywhere in favour of large geographical Divisions — more upheavals! Yet another power struggle developed over the proposal to merge the Eastern and North Eastern Regions, with much lobbying of the Minister against the proposal undertaken by the trade unions. This re-shuffle took two years to implement.

With the passing of the 1968 Transport Act, the requirement to prepare a scheme for the future organisation of the railways was met by inviting McKinsey and Co Inc, to act as consultants. Their recommendation was strongly in favour of appointing a chief executive for the railways, reporting to the Board, something that had been avoided ever since nationalisation. Implementation of this proposal did not altogether go smoothly. First of all, W.G. Thorpe was appointed; he had been a most effective Line Manager and Regional General Manger, rising to be a Vice-Chairman. But (as he himself pointed out to me one day) by becoming also chief executive he was made responsible to himself, which was illogical. The next appointment was a short-lived one terminating over an unfortunate incident. Finally, at the end of the 25 year story, David Bowick, a thoroughly able railway manager, took over the task, supported by a Railway Management Group, composed of headquarters departmental chiefs and Regional General Managers. But of course the power struggle never ends; a Chief Executive and Board Members with functional responsibilities are bound to differ from time to time — tempered on BR by good humour and good personal relationships, for the most part.

McKinseys followed their first report with a second one on 'Field Organisation' which proposed the abolition of the Regions and their replacement by eight or nine 'Territories'. This controversial project was approved in principle by the BRB. Much management time and effort was wasted in planning its implementation, since it was abandoned — for good and sufficient reasons — in January 1975.

Volumes could be written about the balance of power between the Government and the nationalised railways. The original 1948 BTC was a public corporation on the pattern advocated by Herbert Morrison and adopted by him in the creation of London Transport, namely a board of men of ability, given clear powers and duties in the public interest, but left free to run the activity on business lines. The BTC had its own capital stock; it was given only broad directives as to its policy and it was clearly expected to be self-financing and reasonably autonomous.

Hurcomb certainly assumed this independent status. He considered that, as Chairman, he corresponded with the Minister of Transport, not with officials. If he received a letter from Sir Gilmour Jenkins, who had succeeded him as Permanent Secretary of the Ministry, he would pass it to Beevor, as Chief Secretary of the BTC, to answer. He was insistent that BTC officers such as myself who might be summoned to the Ministry, should not accept instructions from civil servants. On returning from any such visits, I would be cross-questioned by Hurcomb, who was always on the alert for any empire-building or moves in the power game by civil servants who had worked under him and about whom his comments were sometimes unflattering!

In fact, my own contacts with the Ministry officials were pleasant; they were almost always helpful and the friction that had occasionally existed with the wartime Railway Executive Committee had practically evaporated. The Ministry had no illusions about the Railway Executive, however, and the Conservative Government's desire to get rid of it and try to restore, for instance, the Great Western Railway was zealously accepted by those civil servants who had to work with the Parliamentary draughtsmen on the 1953 Act.

Sir Brian Robertson enjoyed universal respect in Whitehall: his relations with Ministers and senior civil servants were good, but they could not dispel the niggling doubts that grew and grew as the British Transport Commission slid into deficit. And once the Treasury has agreed to fund an activity from the public purse, it demands some measure of control. Successively, the later Acts which have written down the capital debt of the railways, funded unremunerative passenger services, and provided investment resources, have tightened the grip on the railways exercised in the first instance by senior civil servants in the Ministry of Transport, and in the background by the detached intellectuals exercising their functions in the Treasury. Reviewing the problems of the railways from time to time has become something that the senior civil servants and the top management of BR have to undertake jointly. The precedent for this was the Joint Steering Group set up in 1966, to report jointly to the Minister of Transport and the Chairman of the British Railways Board. It would have been unthinkable in the years immediately following nationalisation, when Hurcomb would have rejected it as unwarranted interference by civil servants.

Chapter 25
Epilogue: Towards the Eighties

In a single volume of moderate length it has not been easy to cover all the main features of British Rail's history in the first 25 years from 1948. And the ensuing years, from 1972 until the present day, were packed with new developments that in total would need another book to receive adequate treatment. Yet it is difficult to close this account without at least a glance into the future.

Although by 1972 BR had been fundamentally changed from the system taken over at nationalisation, many more changes were on the way. First of all, during the 1970s the glamour business — Inter-City — moved from the 100mph standard running speed, so proudly achieved in the 1960s, towards 125mph on the Western Region and the East Coast Main Line, with extensions due to follow as rapidly as authorisations could be screwed out of a niggardly Ministry (later Department) of Transport. And, everlastingly waiting in the wings for the call to appear as the super-star, lurked the Advanced Passenger Train.

The commuter services in London and the South-East were at last being given a shot in the arm, the first major one since the Eastern Region electrifications of the early 1960s and the Southern Region's Kent Coast and Bournemouth electrifications following on in the same decade. The Great Northern suburban scheme, and authority to start with the London Midland's St Pancras-Bedford scheme, together with (at long last) the infusion of some modern-looking inner suburban stock, the Class 508s, into the Southern, were welcome if belated events.

And on the freight side, the attempt to rebuild a wagon-load service after the 1960s had seen its dramatic decline, was meeting some measure of success. It was based on two major developments: use of the TOPS computer on a real-time basis to monitor the service effectively, for the first time; and construction of long-wheelbase covered wagons equipped with the air brake and able to run at 75mph in services christened 'Speedlink'. Wagon-load had declined from 69% of the freight business in 1967 to only 21% in 1977; at this point the tide began to turn, though recovery was slow. The train-load business of mainly bulk goods, though including some items such as motor car components, was holding up well on the foundations established in the 1960s.

Above all, perhaps, the new system of financial support based on aggregated Public Service Obligation payments by the Government — established by the Railways Act, 1974 but in fact conforming to Regulations of the EEC under the Common Transport Policy of the Community — gave a new security and a self-respect to the management which had suffered from years of deficit payments, with their implications, however unjustified, of business failure.

What then were the headaches, the real problems facing BR as the 1980s were entered? Perhaps the most serious was the need for investment to meet the urgent replacement of traction and rolling stock built in the 1950s and 1960s, much of it as part of the Modernisation Plan. In pre-war steam days, 35 years was a widely accepted 'book life' for locomotives and carriages. Many units in those days could run satisfactorily at a much greater age. In LMS days, old Midland Railway locomotives of 60 years ago could be found 'assisting' on main line expresses from time to time, quite effectively. Why had modern equipment such shorter lives?

The main answer must be, higher speeds and much higher utilisation, ie far greater annual mileages; the shorter life of an internal combustion engine compared with a steam engine must also be a factor. The problem was acute in the case of the diesel multiple-units acquired in large numbers between 1955 and 1962, and the electric multiple-units acquired over a wider period; it was also beginning to arise over diesel and electric locomotives, though in a less acute form. Even some of the Mark II main line carriages built in the later 1960s were beginning to give a rough ride on the West Coast Main Line by 1980. (There was a parallel case in Japan where stock built for the 125mph Shinkansen high-speed services was beginning to need complete overhaul after ten years of intensive running, despite the provision of entirely new standard-gauge track designed for continuous high speed.) In Britain the problem was evident not merely in rolling stock but also on the track; a decade and a half of intensive 100mph services had punished the LMR track severely between London, Birmingham, Liverpool and Manchester.

The investment problem of the 1980s might therefore not be related to the introduction of the APT so much as to the refurbishing and replacement of track, locomotives and multiple-unit vehicles that proved to need replacement much earlier than had been foreseen.

Obviously one must ask why the APT, planning for which had started much earlier, was overtaken by the HST as the prime instrument in establishing a new, thoroughly modern and commercially successful type of Inter-City rail service. First of course comes the fact that APT represented a breakthrough into new rail technology, the implications of which were only appreciated gradually, step by (sometimes painful) step. No less than three radical new developments were packed into a single vehicle — the tilting body, the 'self-steering' bogie and the hydro-kinetic brake. Some engineers thought there were too many eggs in one basket. The possible gremlins and teething troubles were so clearly there, that the BRB wisely decided that exhaustive testing must take place, first in the Derby laboratories, then on the special test track at Old Dalby, lastly on the main line. Problems did arise and were successively dealt with: but meanwhile the years were passing.

Policy changes were forced upon BR by British Leyland's decision not to go ahead with the production of the lightweight gas turbine originally envisaged as the APT's motive power and included in the test prototype. The decision to change to electric traction, assisted by the work that the French had done in the improvement of current collection systems for very high speeds, obviously directed the APT towards use on the West Coast Main Line. There was thus a problem of how to achieve high speeds on the other prime routes, the East Coast Main Line and the London to South Wales line, for instance. This gap, providentially, the HST was able to fill.

Underlying the APT concept however there were problems that had certainly been under-estimated in the earlier years. The great attraction of APT to management was the designers' claim that it was a means of achieving very high speeds over existing tracks, and thereby avoiding the need to build an entirely new railway as the Japanese had done with the Tokkaido line and the French were planning with 'Europolitain' (or Paris-Sud-Est). Its overall cost thereby could be, it was argued, kept attractively low.

But in practice APT proved to be not just a train but a rail system. Despite the power of the hydro-kinetic brake, signalling designed for 100mph could not cope with 155mph running. Finding paths for even the pre-war streamliners with 90mph maxima or thereabouts had been difficult; pathing for the APT 50 years later was a still greater headache. There were associated problems of atmospheric pressures when trains passed on tracks with the traditional 'six-foot' spacing between them at combined speeds of 300mph — and also when entering single-line tunnels, or passing trains in double-line tunnels. Despite the high cost of Tokkaido and Paris-Sud-Est, there were many advantages in a purpose-built line on which these problems could be solved at the outset.

Meanwhile the HST came into production relatively quickly and proved an immediate success. Assigned initially to routes upon which the 125mph capacity could be exploited for much of the distance, it was able to reduce journey times significantly, and the new Mark III coaches set a new and higher standard of riding comfort. It was no wonder that there were murmurs to the effect that, in terms of cost-effectiveness, the money that had been poured into the APT project could have been better spent upon more HSTs, coming earlier into service.

But the faith of the BRB and its chief officers in APT was never seen, publicly at any rate, to waver. They refused to accept any comparison with Concorde, any suggestion that BR had hatched a technical marvel but a commercial non-starter. Only the experience of the eighties would show whether this courageous and consistent stand would be vindicated.

Perhaps the other main headaches for BR were those of improving staff productivity and ensuring adequate Government financial support. In a telling study published in 1980, BR produced the results of a comparison between itself and nine other European railways, prepared by a mixed team of transport economists and BR officers. The study established that in this league table, BR showed almost the best financial performance, by the test of the proportion of costs met out of revenue. Conversely, Government support for BR was pretty low by the standards obtaining elsewhere. (Perhaps in consequence, BR's fare levels were high.) British railwaymen worked on average longer hours than their Continental counterparts, but were paid less. Productivity of train crews in passenger working showed BR to be similar to most other railways, but in freight working it was markedly lower, mainly due to the fact that other railways have largely abolished guards and/or drivers' assistants on freight trains.

Here then was a parcel of headaches, together with some encouraging signs, for BR's Chairman, Board Members and top management, not to mention the trade union leaders, as the 1980s opened. The first 25 years had been stormy at times; history was unlikely to repeat itself in the next 25 years, but that they would be eventful could confidently be predicted.

Appendix 1
What the Figures Show: BR after 25 Years

'The figures speak for themselves' is seldom true. Without explanation, most statistics are liable to be misinterpreted or misused. When they span a period as long as 25 years, comparability between different years is often difficult because of organisational changes, or changes in the basis of compilation. This is very true of British Rail, managed successively by the Railway Executive, the British Transport Commission, and the British Railways Board, three bodies with different remits from the Government, and different organisations.

Before 1939, the railway companies produced both financial accounts and statistics in a form approved by the Minister of Transport under statutory powers. They were published in the annual 'Railway Returns' and contained a great deal of useful information.

During the war, for obvious security reasons, publication was discontinued. After the war, summary figures for the war period were published in a single issue, but publication in the full pre-war form was not resumed during the control period which ended only with the nationalisation of the railways on 1 January 1948. The 1938 'Railway Returns' contained 141 pages; the post-war statement covered the years 1938-46 in 34 pages and was produced by the Railway Clearing House with a covering note by the Deputy Secretary of the Ministry of War Transport explaining that, quite apart from security considerations during the war years, 'shortage of staff made it necessary to suspend the collection of some of the information normally kept and to make certain changes in the basis of other particulars. As a result, it is impossible to provide a continuous record covering the war years of all the particulars previously published'.

The BTC, which as the overall financial entity was responsible for the accounts and statistics of all the undertakings under its control, was not required to follow the form of the pre-war statutory returns; but under Section 94 of the Transport Act, 1947, the Minister gave a very broadly worded direction on 27 July 1949 to the Commission about the information to be contained in the accounts and statistics. So far as the railways were concerned, the statistics came under the

227

broad headings of 'assets', 'staff', 'traffic' and 'operations'; but the actual data specified were very basic indeed.

The Comptroller of the BTC, R.H. (later Sir Reginald) Wilson had however been anxious from the outset to ensure that the statistics should be as full and informative as possible. This he had already in fact achieved; in the BTC's first Annual Report, that for 1948, the financial and statistical accounts, with the explanatory notes attached to the figures, occupied no less than 225 pages! The largest component was of course the section relating to the railways.

After 1953 there was some reduction in the information given, following the abolition of the Executives apart from London Transport, though the 1953 Act did not repeal the requirement in the 1947 Act. However, the main reduction came in the Beeching era with the setting up of the British Railways Board. The 1962 Act repealed the Minister's powers to give directions about accounts and statistics conferred by the 1947 Act, and the new British Railways Board considerably 'streamlined' the information published. The accounts and statistics of the BRB for 1966, for instance, occupied only 48 pages. The minimum data listed in the original direction to the BTC were however still provided, though much of the incidental detailed material was now omitted. By 1972 however a good deal less was published, the accounts and statistics having come down to 30 pages, even though the original basic requirements specified in 1949 were still covered.

To measure some of the changes that have taken place in the size and character of British Rail in its first 25 years, statistics for 1 January 1948 and 31 December 1972 are given below under the main headings originally specified by the Minister, with explanatory notes. (Financial results have of course been discussed under 'Money Matters'.)

ASSETS	January 1948	December 1972	Index 1948=100
Route-miles open for traffic	19,639	11,537	59
Track-miles (including sidings)	52,254	30,025	57

This reduction reflects more than anything else the Beeching 'Re-shaping'. Before it, in 1962, route-miles had still been 17,471 and track-miles 47,417. The slight difference in the percentage reduction between route and track reflects the closing of many single-line branches, mitigated by the retention of some lines for freight traffic only, also the reduction in marshalling yards and other sidings, due to the changes in the pattern of freight traffic.

	January 1948	December 1972	Index 1948=100
Stations (passenger & parcels)	1,886	2,198	117
” (passenger & freight)	4,815	182	4
” (freight only)	1,593	386	24
TOTAL	8,294	2,766	33

These figures show the most dramatic effect of Beeching. The apparent rise in 'passenger and parcels' stations is of course entirely due to transfers from the 'passenger and freight' category following withdrawal of freight facilities, which more than offsets the large number of passenger station closures. Other developments include the transfer of the sundries business to National Carriers Ltd after 1968, and the melting-away of the wagon-load freight business, with a concentration upon train-load working, mostly between 'private sidings' such as NCB pits and CEGB power stations, which are the main reasons for the tremendous reductions in freight terminals.

	January 1948	December 1972	Index 1948=100
Marshalling yards (hump)	94	35	37
” ” (flat)	879	89	10
TOTAL	973	124	47

Here again the tremendous changes in the character of BR's freight business, with the virtual disappearance of the bulk of the wagon-load traffic, particularly house coal, is dramatically illustrated.

	January 1948	December 1972
Locomotives (standard gauge)		
Steam	20,023	—
Diesel-electric	53	3,633
Electric	16	317

To compare total locomotive power at the beginning and end of the 25 years is meaningless because of the large-scale introduction of diesel and electric multiple-unit trains or individual power coaches.

	January 1948	December 1972
Passenger carriages		
Loco-hauled	36,033	6,791
EMU stock	4,184	6,747
DMU stock	40	3,467
	40,257	17,005

The reduction reflects mainly improved utilisation of stock of all classes, largely due to diesel and electric traction achieving much greater daily mileages with much shorter turn-rounds at terminals (often involving problems of cleaning and servicing stock). It also reflects the drastic reduction in the stock formerly retained to meet seasonal peaks, mainly the summer holiday season.

	January 1948	December 1972	Index 1948=100
Freight vehicles			
Open merchandise	323,609	32,861	10
Covered "	146,873	34,194	23
Mineral	684,886	170,052	25
Steel carrying ⎱	68,266	⎧ 25,323	46
Other ⎰		⎩ 6,122	
TOTAL	1,223,634	268,552	22

Here again the changes are dramatic. In minerals, the 1948 figures include some 544,000 former private owners' wagons vested in the BTC on nationalisation, many of which were of small capacity with grease lubrication, and were scrapped as soon as possible. The reduction in house coal traffic and also the marked increase in the size of new wagons built after 1948 were major factors leading to the reduction in the size of the fleet.

The fitting of continuous brakes enabled the number of brake vans to be reduced, quite apart from the fall in the number of trains operated.

The reduction in the number of covered vans was noticeably less than in the case of open merchandise wagons, reflecting changes in the nature of the traffic carried.

	1948	1972	Index 1948=100
OPERATIONS			
Loaded train miles (million)			
Passenger & parcels	220.2	195.6	89
Freight	118.4	53.0	45

The transformation in the scale of BR's freight business is illustrated by the following figures:-

	1948	1972	Index 1948=100
Estimated net freight ton-miles (millions)	21,456	12,858	60

If the volume of business fell, the efficiency with which it was conducted improved, judged by the standard of wagon loading.

	1948	1972	Index 1948=100
Average wagon load at starting point, in tons			
Coal and coke	10.92	18.90	173
All traffic	7.95	19.79	249

Increase in the size of wagons was one major factor; another was the loss of so much general merchandise, sundries and smalls traffic, and its replacement by a concentration upon bulk traffics.

	1948	1972	Index 1948=100
Passenger journeys (000s)	996,050	753,608	76

There were some changes in average distance travelled, but the basis of compilation had changed. Season tickets however were comparable, and the average length of these journeys rose from 12.76 miles to 17.17 miles.

	January 1948	December 1972	Index 1948=100
STAFF			
Railway	542,829	196,635	36

The above figures excluded in both cases the staff employed in the locomotive, carriage and wagon main workshops, which by 1972 had been transferred to BR Engineering Ltd. Unfortunately deducting 'workshop' staff in 1948 involves taking out also staff employed in Regional maintenance centres who were not subsequently transferred to BREL, and the 1948 figure is therefore slightly under-stated.

Furthermore, the 1948 figures include road collection and delivery staff not shown separately in the 'Railway Staff Census: Analysis of Persons Employed by Principal Grades' who were, together with certain goods terminals staff, transferred to National Carriers Ltd under the 1968 Transport Act. Direct comparison is thus not exactly possible.

	January 1948	December 1972	Index 1948=100
Railway Workshops (Loco, carriage & wagon)	84,809	33,001	39

These figures reflect the contraction in the railway workshops due partly to rationalisation and closing of smaller shops, partly to higher productivity from mechanisation.

Overall, the drop in the railways' staff results from the combined operation of a number of factors. First of all, of course, comes the contraction in the scale of the railway business and of the assets employed. Then comes the effect of 'versatility' or 'productivity' agreements, such as the Windsor and Penzance agreements. Lastly, there is the effect of organisational changes; for instance, the transfer of road transport staff, included in the 1948 figures, to NCL with consequent exclusion from the 1972 figures. (In 1948 the figures exclude the former railway police, and staff employed in electricity generation, who would not appear in 1972 in any case because of the formation of the British Transport police and the closing down of BTC generating stations in favour of buying traction current from the CEGB.)

The 1972 figures show separately the staff employed in property management, (1014) who are included under 'railway' in 1948. There is also a figure of staff (mainly salaried) for 'corporate and common services' at BRB headquarters, totalling 4,322, which does not of course equate with the BTC figure of 'administrative, technical and clerical' staff employed on the railways in 1948, who are included in 'railway' staff above.

These notes illustrate the size of the reduction in railway staff, but also the difficulty and indeed the danger of making detailed comparisons.

Appendix 2

Bibliography and Sources

Historians have good cause to be thankful to Sir Cyril (Lord) Hurcomb for the extremely full and informative Annual Reports of the British Transport Commission between 1948 and 1952. (The Railway Executive did produce its own Annual Report for 1948 but was rebuked for doing so and instructed that, like the other Executives, its duty was to contribute a section to the BTC document.)

The early Reports are very much occupied with administrative and organisational matters arising out of the 1947 Transport Act. Their financial sections are particularly detailed and informative. After 1953, under the chairmanship of Sir Brian Robertson, the Reports are rather shorter and the emphasis changes; manpower and investment questions tend to dominate the text.

Yet another change took place after the demise of the Commission. Under Dr Beeching, the Annual Reports of the British Railways Board gave more prominence to commercial policy and economic factors. The financial and statistical statements became noticeably abridged compared with the voluminous data provided by the BTC.

Under Sir Stanley Raymond and Sir Henry Johnson, the re-adjustment to the new role of the railways after the changes of the 1960s dominates the Annual Reports. Finally, in 1972, under (Sir) Richard Marsh, the Report becomes a public relations exercise, skilfully designed and profusely illustrated — a 'glossy' that is a far cry from the massive, sober volumes of 1948-52.

Various writers have dealt at length with the economic problems of the railways, so much so that there is an acute problem of selection. D.H. Aldcroft's *British Railways in Transition* is a study by an economic historian that concentrates on railways, whereas treatises by other academics — C.D. Foster and K. Gwilliam in particular — deal with the whole field of transport policy. Many writers concentrating on railways have had an axe to grind which somewhat detracts from the value of their work; but G. Freeman Allen's *British Rail After Beeching* is well-informed and objective.

Studies of mechanical engineering are legion but notable is *British Railways Engineering 1948-80* by Johnson and Long.

For an account of railway industrial relations with particular reference to the manning and productivity negotiations, there is *All Change* by C.S. McLeod, who was BR's Chief Industrial Relations Officer during some of the most important years.

Lively accounts of personal experiences under nationalisation are very variable in historical value, but G.F. Fiennes: *I Tried to Run a Railway* and A.J. Pearson: *Man of the Rail* are both illuminating.

Organisational changes up to 1971 are dealt with in my own book *The Organisation of British Railways*.

Needless to say, the files of the railway journals — *Railway Gazette* and *Modern Railways* in particular — are full of interesting material, while another valuable point of view can be extracted from the files of *Railway Review*, the journal of the National Union of Railwaymen. Until its demise in 1964, *Modern Transport* offered many well-informed articles also.

Index

References are not given to the bodies that have successively managed the undertaking of 'British Railways' — the Railway Executive, the British Transport Commission and the British Railways Board — as these are constantly mentioned throughout the text, and the principal subjects dealt with are indicated by the chapter headings. The same applies to the individual Regions of BR.